SUSTAINABLE

THE WAR ON FREE ENTERPRISE, PRIVATE PROPERTY AND INDIVIDUALS

TOM DEWEESE

GOLD DUST PUBLISHING

For information about permission to reproduce selections from this book, write to contact@gdustpublishing.com or to Permissions, Gold Dust Publishing, 3126 W. Cary St STE 235 Richmond, VA 23221

Library of Congress Cataloging-In-Publication Data is available
ISBN 978-1-7320370-0-7 (Paperback)
ISBN 978-1-7320370-1-4 (Ebook)
ISBN 978-1-7320370-2-1 (Hardback)
1.1

Cover design by Andrea Ho

To order additional copies of this book please visit
www.sustainabledevelopment.com

CONTENTS

OVERVIEW

This book is a beginning for the many Americans who know little or nothing about the threat of Sustainable Development and how it affects their future.

I have not attempted to tell everything about this issue. To do so would take a multi-volume encyclopedia set. Therefore, I haven't included subjects such as population control, health care, full details on smart meters, the public education system, or the role Sustainable Development plays in creating a total surveillance society. That information certainly exists and I have addressed it all in other writings.

However, here I decided to provide the basics so that even the new reader is able to wrap their head around this massive issue. In addition, I fully believe that it isn't necessary to know every detail to fight Sustainable Development because, as I point out in the book, if private property rights can be fully protected, then Sustainable Development can be stopped in its tracks. So, that's the focus of this book.

This book can be a valuable tool for elected officials attempting to understand the origins and the inevitable results of policies being forced on them. In addition, focusing on protecting property rights is the best advice for local and state activists who want to fight it.

Sustainable: The War on Free Enterprise, Private Property, and Individuals details how an outside force can create a plan to take over the world by gaining the assistance of its intended victims. It's happening in every nation of the world, in every state of our nation, and in every community. It is eating our freedoms like a cancer. It is evil. And it must be stopped. This book is where to learn how to do it.

ACKNOWLEDGEMENTS

The information in this book comes from many sources. I have spent more that twenty years studying this issue. I want to specifically thank certain individuals without whom this book would not be possible. First, the man who first opened my eyes and taught me about Agenda 21 and Sustainable Development was the late Henry Lamb. He attended international UN meetings and learned of the scheme. He then taught me and many others what it all meant. His passing was a great tragedy to the freedom movement in American. Next, I thank Dr. Michael Coffman. I value the experience of having traveled the nation with him, speaking out about these issues. He was an invaluable and fierce warrior in this fight. He too, has passed on. I will miss his irreplaceable wisdom and knowledge. I deeply appreciate the insight provided by expert Ric Frost on the dangers of Conservation Easements, and thank him for allowing me to use his information in the book. Equally, I thank John Anthony for providing much of the information on the HUD AFFH program and on the dangers of Regional government. John is a powerhouse of information. I also thank Shu Bartholomew for her excellent input on Homeowners Associations. She is one of the nation's leading experts on HOAs and has been exposing that threat for several years through her radio show called On the Commons.   I thank activist Johnnelle Raines for her unwavering dedication to the fight for freedom. She and hundreds like her across the nation are the reason we still have a chance to fight. Finally, I thank my incredible team of Kathleen Marquardt and CJ Scrofani, without whom this book would not be possible. Kathleen's own wide knowledge of this subject was invaluable as she made suggestions and added vital information along with the laborious job of editing and creating the index. Together, CJ and I developed the concept for the book and the battle plan to go with it. He is simply my rock!

THE ENEMY WITHIN

"At what point shall we expect the approach of danger? By what means shall we fortify against it? Shall we expect some trans-Atlantic military giant to step the ocean, and crush us at a blow?

Never!

All the armies of Europe, Asia, and Africa combined, … could not by force, take a drink from the Ohio, or make a track on the Blue Ridge, in a trial of a thousand years.

At what point then is the approach of danger to be expected?

I answer, if it ever reach us, it must spring up amongst us. It cannot come from abroad. If destruction be our lot, we ourselves must be its author and finisher. As a nation of free men, we must live through all times, or die by suicide."

Abraham Lincoln
Address before the Young Men's Lyceum
Springfield, Illinois – January 27, 1838

CHAPTER ONE

PROSPERITY - STABILITY - FREEDOM
WHY PRIVATE PROPERTY MATTERS

Most Americans tend to think of private property simply as a home -- the place where the family resides, stores their belongings and finds shelter and safety from the elements. It's where you live. It's yours because you pay the mortgage and the taxes. Most people don't give property ownership much more thought than that.

There was a time when property ownership was considered to be much more. Property, and the ability to own and control it, was life itself. The great economist, John Locke, whose writings and ideas had major influence on the nation's founders, believed that "life and liberty are secure only so long as the right of property is secure."

John Locke advocated that if property rights did not exist then the incentive for an industrious person to develop and improve property would be destroyed; that the industrious person would be deprived of the fruits of his labor; that marauding bands would confiscate by force the goods produced by others; and that mankind would be impelled to remain on a bare-subsistence level of hand to mouth survival because the accumulation of anything of value would invite attack.

In short, human civilization would be reduced to the level of a pack of wolves and cease to exist because lack of control over your own actions caused fear and insecurity. Private property ownership, Locke argued, brought stability and wealth to individuals, leading to a prosperous society of man.

One only has to look to the example of the former Soviet Union to see clearly what happens to a society when an outlaw government exercises brute force to take control of private property. Under that tyrannical government, each of Locke's predictions came true there.

The Russian Revolution of 1917 was easy to exploit and control by the Communists because the people were oppressed as their actions, labors, and living conditions were under the control of an all-powerful kingdom. The Czarist rule had been passed on from generation to generation through birthright rather than by the choice of the people. As a result, a ruling class emerged based on relationship with the Czars. The ruling class could decide at will to take property, select industry and destroy lives. This led to wealth and power for a few. There was a middle class made up mainly of the bakers, the shopkeepers and tradesmen. With their modest incomes they were able to afford simple homes. The rest of the population was left in poverty; their survival was at the whim of the elite.

The Soviet Revolution promised the poor that it would throw out the ruling class and in its place create a government controlled by the people. There would be decent housing, jobs, and food enough for all. All would be equal. The wealthy would be banished and their riches shared throughout the land. The Communists promised "freedom" to the masses.

"A Marxist category called the 'Middle Class' consists of people who are 'numb, bewildered, and scared, into silence' and whose lives are tedious.' To engage a revolution the 'middle class' must be targeted with an appeal for hope."

Saul Alinsky - Marxist

Of course the opposite occurred because the Communists were simply using the frustrations and emotions of the oppressed to win their favor. Throughout its history, the Soviet government excused its every action under the banner of equality for all. There were no property rights, no freedom of enterprise, and no protections of individual actions. Instead, the Soviet government enforced redistribution of wealth schemes, confiscating homes from the rich and middle class. Many times it forced owners to share the homes with multiple families, destroying the right of ownership and control. Eventually, with no one responsible for the upkeep, the properties fell into disrepair.

As Soviet economic policies eliminated the profit motive from the market, the incentive to produce was eliminated. Everyone, producer and non-producer alike, was reduced to an identical government handout. This is what the Soviets called equality. Soon the producers learned they could produce less, yet still get their government stipend. As a result, the shelves of the stores were rendered bare and, eventually, the economy collapsed and society sank into despair.

Nonetheless, the propaganda of the glorious "Workers' Paradise" of the Soviet Union was used throughout the world as a blueprint to create new revolutions; Eastern Europe, East Germany, parts of Asia, Africa and Cuba all fell for the illusion of equality and freedom. In fact, the promised equality became the reality as all became equally poor when jobs, food and services collapsed under the assault on private property, free enterprise and individuality.

The same basic redistribution schemes of the Soviets were later used by Zimbabwe's former dictator Robert Mugabe to destroy that agriculturally-rich African nation. Mugabe confiscated farmland owned by white farmers and gave it to friends of his corrupt government – most of whom had never even seen a farm. The result was economic disaster, widespread poverty, and hunger in a land that had once fed the continent. It's interesting to note that in the days before he was finally overthrown, Mugabe was begging the owners to return to run the farms again while he begged for $1.5 billion in food aid to prevent mass starvation. It's the classic result of every totalitarian power grab.

Most recently the South American nation of Venezuela, rich in natural resources, has been reduced to poverty and despair by redistribution of wealth through murderous taxes and confiscation of private businesses and homes. Once again, shelves in stores are bare of goods while parents are actually being forced to give up their children because they can no longer afford to feed them.

Clearly John Locke's warnings have been vindicated. Private property ownership is much more than a house. It is the root of a prosperous, healthy, human society based on the individual's freedom to live a life of his own, gaining from the fruits of his own labor. Take that option away and the people always react the same way. They stop producing.

Using Locke's ideas as their guide, the Founders of the United States of America created a system of government designed to protect private property and the free enterprise system that grew from the ability of free individuals to freely produce their goods and services. The nation prospered like none before it. Nowhere else in history were citizens able to improve their lives and have the opportunity to build individual wealth as in America. It didn't matter if you were born poor, were basically uneducated, or lacked the "proper" contacts or pedigree.

Though no one is guaranteed to be successful and prosperous, at least here in America each individual was assured the right and the freedom to try. It was the chief reason why people from other nations poured into America. **Hope. Opportunity. Freedom.** The words became synonymous with the very image of America. Streets paved in gold! Freedom! **The American dream.**

Why were Americans different in the eyes of the world? Because they had a different idea for how mankind was to live. A philosophy based on the ideal of individual liberty. An optimism created by ideas never before considered by government. No kings. No potentates. No dictators. Just individuals, free to produce. Why? Because the people owned and controlled their own land which provided them the ability to build personal wealth. No King had ever allowed such a thing.

From the very beginning, the United States was guided by the idea of private property ownership. It was written into our governing documents. Property and freedom. One cannot survive without the other.

James Madison, the father of the Constitution, said, "*As a man is said to have a right to his property, he may be equally said to have a property in his rights.*"(Meaning that even if a person owned nothing else, he still owned his rights, which is the most valuable property of all.)

Founding Father John Adams said: "*The moment the idea is admitted into society that property is not as sacred as the laws of God, and that there is not a force of law and public justice to protect it, anarchy and tyranny commence.*"

These lofty ideas stayed with America throughout its history. In the early part of the Twentieth Century, President Calvin Coolidge expressed the same ideals when he said: "*Ultimately, property rights and personal rights are the same thing.*"

Later, author and philosopher, Ayn Rand, who had grown up under the tyranny of the Soviet Union, and knew first hand how the destruction of property rights condemned man to live in a state of misery and hopelessness, wrote: "The right to life is the source of all rights – and the right to property is their only implementation. Without property rights, no other rights are possible. Since man has to sustain his life by his own efforts, the man who has no right to the product of his efforts has no means to sustain his life. The man who produces while others dispose of his product, is a slave."

Yet, in spite of all of the best laid plans of the Founders, regardless of the incredible history of success from those plans, the poison of failed Socialism has begun to seep into the cracks of the American foundation. Today, the once unique design of citizen control over the American government is losing ground. Government has begun to break out of its legal restraints as it rushes to rule, regulate and interfere in nearly every individual's life decisions. As prosperity fades and the people become more desperate for their personal survival, the ideals of property and freedom diminish in the minds of many, in exchange for a false security.

Even as history has shown not a single socialist/communist success, rather a legacy of broken promises, poverty, misery, and the inevitable tyranny that follows, the Siren's Song continues to draw in its desperate believers. And it's gaining steam. Where once the tyranny of top-down government control applied to the conquest of only one nation at a time, a brave new world is rushing toward the promise of a single global overseer armed with those same, well-worn empty promises -- that the elimination of free enterprise, individuality and private property will somehow lead to equality, eradication of poverty and some kind of undefined freedom. What such promises really lead to is an all-powerful government tyranny.

CHAPTER TWO

THERE IS ONLY ONE SOLUTION TO POVERTY AND IT'S NOT GOVERNMENT

Eradicating poverty is the most popular excuse for the expansion of government power. It's a crisis! Someone must do something! How can a civilized people allow their fellow humans to go hungry?

The statistics on global poverty are staggering. According to the United Nation's Millennium Project, there are currently 1.2 billion people living in poverty. Fifty thousand deaths per day occur worldwide as a result of poverty. Every year more than ten million children die of hunger and preventable diseases. More than half of the world's population lives on less than $2 per day and 800 million people go to bed hungry every night.

As a result of the constant drumbeat to "do something," there are countless efforts underway to focus attention on poverty. To combat the situation, there are major programs run by churches and charitable organizations to promote themselves through dramatic television commercials that tug at our hearts to "take action today!" Meanwhile local, state, federal, and international government programs promise to eradicate poverty. Massive amounts of foreign aid dollars have been distributed to countries around the world to help feed the poor. Poverty reduction targets have been set. International goals have been announced. Deadlines have been determined. Agreement that poverty must be eradicated has been reached by every national leader in the world.

And what is the government's most preferred way to eliminate poverty? Redistribution of wealth. It's the force behind the UN's Agenda 2030 and its drive for Social Justice. In fact, redistribution schemes are the common excuse behind nearly every government poverty program as well as most private charitable programs.

Billions of dollars have been sucked from the pockets of citizens by way of taxes, always under the altruistic excuse of helping the poor. Poverty program schemes are all the same -- tax money from the producers and give that money to the non-producers. Yet, as billions of dollars are taken for the "cause," poverty steadily increases. Little progress, if any, has been achieved as poverty continues to escalate. In fact, there is an ever-growing disparity between rich and poor.

For well over one hundred years, governments and charities have been focused on rushing aid to the poor and starving. Yet none of these efforts addresses the basic reason why poverty exists in the first place. The solutions, which call for more and more aid, simply respond to the visual effects of poverty such as starvation, ignorance, and poor health. None truly address the cause. As a result, rather than easing the situation, the number of poor continues to grow.

Most of the current anti-poverty efforts focus on redistributing funds from wealthier nations to poorer ones, either through mandatory taxation or charitable donations. This system ignores the fact that tomorrow the poor need to be fed again. Taxpayers, or the voluntary donor, must dig into their own funds again and again to help. The process is repeated daily, each time the poor recipient is only temporarily helped, as the taxpayers or the donors become poorer themselves.

Meanwhile, as massive funds are moved in and out of governments, ever-growing bureaucracies are institutionalized to run the system. Eventually, more money goes to feed the machinery of poverty than actually gets into the hands of the intended poor. Such a system *sustains* poverty rather than eradicating it. Interestingly, with each new program, government becomes larger and more powerful.

In short, no matter how much is taxed and spent to eradicate the problem, the result is that we have more poor! In truth, the promise of eradicating poverty is a growth industry – the "Compassion Cartel." The more poverty in the world, the more powerful and rich the Cartel becomes. What possible incentive does it have to actually stop poverty?

THE REAL WAY TO END POVERTY AND BUILD PERSONAL EMPOWERMENT

If one truly wants to help eliminate poverty, perhaps it's time to re-think the process. To begin, one should ask this question – why are some nations (and individuals) wealthy and others are so poor?

The reason the United States has led the world in wealth, standard of living, and abundance is that every resident of the United States has had the ability and the opportunity to invest and produce their own capital and build personal wealth. Why is that possible? And why has most of the rest of the world failed, and continues to fail, at such an attempt? The answer is actually very simple. The United States created a very easy, immediate, complete system for recording and securing ownership of all private property in the nation. In truth, this system makes the County Recorder's office in every community in the United States the most powerful force of freedom in the world. In short, those records of ownership of all property provide proof of individual ownership. That proof of ownership is the root to building personal wealth, which leads to individual empowerment.

Peruvian economist Hernando deSoto explains the root of American wealth in his book, *The Mystery of Capital.* DeSoto asks, "Why does Capitalism thrive only in the West, as if enclosed in a bell jar?"

"Capital," he argues, "is the force that raises the productivity of labor and creates the wealth of nations. It is the lifeblood of the capitalist system, the foundation of progress, and the one thing that the poor countries of the world cannot seem to produce for themselves."

Why not in other countries? Because the laws and practices of most countries in the world make it nearly impossible for average citizens to own and prove ownership of property. There are vast obstacles to gaining legal ownership. For example:

» In Mexico it takes twenty years before a piece of property can be recorded.
» In Peru, it took de Soto's team of experts 289 days to legally register a new business, even after paying over $1,200 in registration fees.
» In the Philippines a prospective property owner would first have to organize an association with his neighbors in order to qualify for a state housing finance program. The entire process could take 168 steps, involving 53 public and private agencies, taking 13 to 25 years. And so it goes in country after country.

The impact of a $1,200 fee in a poor nation is enough to forever discourage even the attempt to register property. In many developing countries such an amount may equal an entire year's income.

In addition, it's important to note the impact free markets and private property have on the income of a nation's citizens. The per capita income for Americans is $41,400 per year. For Europeans, where more government control is exercised, the per capita income is $27,400. In the former Communist nations of Eastern Europe, now that free markets have been established, it's now $3,295; yet, just a few years ago it was $2,047. As more freedom and greater ability to own property grows, so does the per capita income.

If ownership of property cannot be properly recorded and able to be traced directly to the owner, then it cannot create equity and cannot be used as collateral for credit. Thus the property is not, then, of value to the owner; it becomes nothing more than an expense. This situation has created, in deSoto's estimate, over $9.3 trillion in "dead capital," i.e. property that cannot be used by anyone to create equity and therefore wealth. Without the ability to use it for productive purposes it's useless – dead.

While it's common practice in the United States for individuals to buy property, hold it for a few years, and sell it at a substantial profit or move up to a better home, thereby creating personal wealth, such a system is basically unheard of in most nations of the world. If one doesn't have, or can't prove title to a piece of property, then no bank will make loans on that property. In nations where property cannot be easily and legally registered, the only recourse is to go to friends and relatives, get a smaller loan (thereby reducing one's ability to build a company) and still never have title to the property or to the business or its inventory. Though people may live on and pay for property for years, it is hidden in an underground economy not beneficial to the individual or the national economy because ownership cannot be proven.

"In the West, by contrast," deSoto argues, "every parcel of land, every building, every piece of equipment, or store of inventory is represented in a property document that is the visible sign of a vast hidden process that connects all these assets to the rest of the economy." Seventy percent of all small businesses in the United States are started by equity loans on personal homes. Small, independently-owned businesses employ the majority of people in the U.S.

This, then, is the hidden secret of why the West became so wealthy and much of the rest of the world has been mired in poverty. **Obviously poverty can never be eradicated – and will actually increase – until government gets out of the way and everyone has equal opportunity to own and benefit from the wealth associated with private property ownership.**

Today's poor in undeveloped nations certainly want the same opportunities to advance, yet many now live in societies that are in some ways

3,000 years behind the modern world. Because of its system of private property ownership, the West created a world of advanced technology, health, education, and leisure where life expectancy increased each decade. In the West, people truly pursued a life of happiness.

Eradication of poverty in the world won't come from endless aid programs designed to provide mere subsistence. Nor will it come from simply providing jobs. The answer to poverty will come only from providing to all people in the world the tools necessary to create new, independent wealth. Only then will they be able to achieve personal empowerment and live lives of individual independence.

CHAPTER THREE

THE LOST DEFINITION OF PRIVATE PROPERTY RIGHTS

The increasing encroachment of government regulations, pontificating politicians and the enforcement of Social Justice schemes have led to a loss of understanding of the terms private property and property rights. Once it was understood that the unauthorized entering of private property was a violation to the utmost. The property owner was justified and supported in taking necessary actions to remove the trespasser and secure that land.

Today, such ideas in the new America are considered radical, old fashioned, out of touch, and even reprehensible. The homeowner can be arrested for defending against an armed intruder. The intruder can actually sue a homeowner for shooting them even as they break down the door intending to rob and do harm. Home protection is called violence, perhaps even racism. It's a whole new world of compliance, fear, and acceptance rather than pride, protection, and prosperity in ownership.

So, if we are to succeed in restoring the ideals of property ownership and benefit from its given creation of prosperity and freedom, then a short discussion of the full definition of private property is in order.

When you purchase property, how much of the land do you own? What is the depth of the soil? Do you own the water on the land? Do you own the air above it? As property rights expert, Dr. Timothy Ball wrote, "All these questions speak to political issues that transcend private, regional and national boundaries. Nationally and internationally, lack of this knowledge is being exploited by those who seek control…"

In the beginning of the nation – after the Declaration of Independence and the American Revolution, and the signing of the Treaty of Paris with Great Britain -- the American people became complete, sovereign freeholders in the land with the same prerogatives as the King once had. Now in this new nation the English King had no further claim to the land and could not tax or otherwise encumber it.

From that point the United States government acknowledged private ownership by issuing land patents, also called "Letter Patents." They were signed by the President of the United States and recorded in the county record. From that point the land then became the owner's property in a "true land title." There were no other claims on the land. Land Patents or "Allodial Titles" were one of the major motivators of the American Revolution, providing rights to the land, free and clear of the liens and encumbrances of the King of England.

Land Patents are a contract or Document of Title, issued by a government or state for the conveyance of some portion of land from the public domain to private individuals. According to Black's Law, a Land Patent Contract means the complete and absolute ownership of land; a paramount and individual right of property in land.

But, as expert Ron Gibson has written, the enjoyment of free and clear title allowing owners to "own" their land without interference from any government, including the government of the United States, didn't last long. Writes Gibson, "As a result of generations of constructive Trust Fraud perpetuated against the American people. . . we've been conned into believing we are 'owning' property, when in fact, and by law, we're only in 'possession' of property utilizing it as a renter or tenant would. So long as we pay our rent (i.e., taxes and mortgages), get the licenses, pay the fees, have it insured, regulated, zoned and permitted, we can still remain 'in possession.'"

Gibson goes on to say, "Our Land Patent Laws were largely derived from Old English Laws, knows as Allodial Patents, which means (The King of your Land). Once a patent has been issued by the United States Government and signed by the President of the United States, and recorded in the county recorders records in which the land is located, it then becomes your fee simple title (owing to no one). Meaning a true land title!"

Today, this history has been largely ignored by our government. Instead of a Land Patent or Allodial Patent issued when one buys property, we are issued a Warranty Deed. That is not a true title, but rather a "color of title." That means you have a partner in the ownership of the land. The partner is the State, which encumbers the property with taxes and liens and all of those things, which simply render you a tenant on what should be your own land.

And therein lies the root of the misconception mentioned in the opening chapter, that property is just the place where we live. The government's refusal to acknowledge true property rights has led to a massive destruction of the American system, and is at the root of the creation of the largest reorganization of human society ever attempted.

In the 1990s, an all-out assault on property rights was well underway, lead by a radical environmental movement, resulting in massive federal land grabs in the name of conservation. As one can imagine, courts across the nation were flooded with cases of people attempting to defend their property rights from government takings. In the state of Washington, one of the major targets for such programs, the state Supreme Court realized it didn't have an adequate definition of property rights to use in considering such cases. That's when State Supreme Court Justice Richard B. Sanders wrote a "Fifth Amendment" treatise which included the following definition of property rights.

"Property in a thing consists not merely in its ownership and possession, but in the unrestricted right of use, enjoyment, and disposal. Anything which destroys any of the elements of property, to that extent, destroys the property itself. The substantial value of property lies in its use. If the right of use be denied, the value of the property is annihilated and ownership is rendered a barren right."

Clearly Sanders' definition is based on the concept of Land Patents and Allodial Title. "Use" of the land is the key. Using the land in a productive way beneficial to the owner is what gives the land value. Simply paying the taxes and mortgage while some undefined government entity can rule and regulate how the property is used, according to Justice Sanders, is a "barren right" that annihilates its value.

So, if private property rights are to be saved in the nation that practically invented the concept, let there be no doubt in what the term means.

TEN POINTS TO DEFINE TRUE PRIVATE PROPERTY RIGHTS

» The owner's exclusive authority to determine how private property is used;
» The owner's peaceful possession, control, and enjoyment of his/her lawfully purchased, real private property;

» The owner's ability to make contracts to sell, rent, or give away all or part of the lawfully purchased/real private property;

» That local, city, county, state, and federal governments are prohibited from exercising eminent domain for the sole purpose of acquiring lawfully purchased/real private property so as to resell to a private interest or generate revenues;

» That no local, city, county, state, or federal government has the authority to impose directives, ordinances, fees, or fines regarding aesthetic landscaping, color selections, tree and plant preservation, or open spaces on lawfully purchased/real private property;

» That no local, city, county, state, or federal government shall implement a land use plan that requires any part of lawfully purchased/real private property be set aside for public use or for a Natural Resource Protection Area directing that no construction or disturbance may occur;

» That no local, city, county, state, or federal government shall implement a law or ordinance restricting the number of outbuildings that may be placed on lawfully purchased/real private property;

» That no local, city, county, state, or federal government shall alter or impose zoning restrictions or regulations that will devalue or limit the ability to sell lawfully purchased/real private property;

» That no local, city, county, state, or federal government shall limit profitable or productive agriculture activities by mandating and controlling what crops and livestock are grown on lawfully purchased/real private property;

» That no local, city, county, state, or federal government representatives or their assigned agents may trespass on private property without the consent of the property owner or is in possession of a lawful warrant from a legitimate court of law. This includes invasion of property rights and privacy by government use of unmanned drone flights, with the exceptions of exigent circumstances such as protection of life, limb or the private property itself.

These points speak specifically to the right of use of the property. They do not infringe on a local government's ability for local rule or to impose local, reasonable, legal zoning policy, so long as such policies recognize and protect the owner's use of their private property.

Under current policies being implemented in every state and nearly every community, each of these points are being violated daily. Local governments are creating partnerships with private developers, using the powers of eminent domain to confiscate property for the building of private entities and enterprises such as shopping malls, manufacturing plants, and housing developments with the express purpose of raising tax revenues.

Federal agencies such as HUD, EPA and Bureau of Land Management (BLM) are systematically fining property owners, even confiscating and locking away private land, prohibiting its use and destroying traditional industry and farming.

State and local governments are forcing developers to set aside large tracts of land to enforce open space and green areas, which imposes punitive financial impositions on the property owners.

Finally, governments at every level routinely trespass on private land to measure, photograph and map, **with the express purpose of creating new regulations.**

Each of these actions is taken by government for the sole purpose of controlling the use of the land. The very idea of "unrestricted right of use" by the property owner terrifies the powers in charge as they race to control every inch of land and its use. Meanwhile, under such plans the very idea of private property rights have become ignored and voided by government edict. The owner, then, has no ability to defend his property, or control who has access. The result is that *private property rights, according to Justice Sanford's definition, have ceased to exist.*

Nearly an unlimited variety of government programs, schemes and tricks are employed to control land use and violate the concept of private property. There are international rules and treaties, federal regulations and programs, state projects, and local plans -- many interconnected to one specific goal designed to change our society, form of government, and way of life. Each focuses on control or destruction of private property to achieve its goal. Leading that drive are powerful forces in partnership with private organizations having specific agendas and nearly unlimited funds effecting and affecting policies necessary for bringing it about.

To preserve our freedom it is vital that every American understand who is behind such a reorganization of our society, why it is being done, and – especially how.

CHAPTER FOUR

THE REORGANIZATION OF HUMAN SOCIETY

There has always been some kind of force loose in the world seeking domination over others. Usually it's a drive for power for power's sake. Conquer other tribes, kingdoms or nations. Grab their resources. Enslave their people. Build wealth and power. Kings saw it as their duty. Megalomaniacs like Napoleon, Hitler, and Stalin lusted for control and power to satisfy their hatred, mistrust, and insecurities. Secret societies have plotted global control for their cause, however demented it might be. Each tried to gain power in different ways. And each eventually failed. In some cases they just pushed too far. Or they miscalculated the weather conditions during their attacks. It's incredible to note that historically both Napoleon and Hitler failed to remember that Russia has a severe winter. In most cases, however, they simply failed to take into account that people facing such oppression fight back more passionately when their homeland and families are threatened.

However, what if such power-mongers could find a way to keep their aggression under wraps, out of sight from those they intend to conquer – until it was too late? Better yet, what if they could actually get their targeted victims to help them achieve that goal to control them? No armies in the field. No shots fired. Instead, they quietly pull in the Trojan Horse and celebrate its arrival. Crazy, you say? Well, not so fast…

What if there was a way for a small, powerful group to rule the world by simply organizing it under a single unifying plan, accepted by nearly everyone as fact and necessary? Through such a process, the people would be convinced that to oppose the plan would be a direct threat to humanity. Acceptance of the plan would see every nation voluntarily surrendering its independence and sovereignty to the aggressors. National leaders would even raise money to pay for the aggressors' system of control. The new rulers would issue the exact process to be followed by all, assuring more and more power with each dictate. Eventually, as the process took hold, people would voluntarily forget their history, reject their culture and never ask questions about it. "Was it not always so?" they would later ask.

What could be such a threat, so powerful that the entire world would lay down to accept such global servitude? **How about the threat of Environmental Armageddon!**

Who could be opposed to saving the planet? What if one dared to oppose such a plan? "I'm free! I'm independent! I have rights," you would claim, holding up a copy of the Constitution. However, the mob, fearing such dangerous ideas, would surround you and rip up your Constitution as it shouted, "It doesn't matter how many rights you think you have if you don't have a planet to stand on! Only selfish zealots who refuse to give up their creature comforts would oppose efforts to save Mother Earth!" Therein would be the end of the debate as the accepted 'truth' was settled. Your new rulers would look on satisfied as their drive for control was complete. Without firing a shot, without an army in the field, and looked upon as heroes and saviors of the planet, they would now be in control of all of the world's resources – the land, the air, the water and the people. Such a force of power would leave little ability for opposition. World domination would be complete.

In truth, there is such a plan for world domination and it is rapidly taking over at a pace and on a scope that no force of power ever experienced in history. So powerful and controlling is this force that, so far, it certainly hasn't had to fire a shot as it gains new power every day. The incredible part about it is that it's no secret. Everyone in the world knows about it. The aggressors have written down every detail of their plan and have told us in their own words how it is to work. People throughout the world – the direct target of the plan – accept each new dictate in its name as most nations enthusiastically help to put it into placed.

The Club of Rome, one of the leading forces behind the scheme openly admitted their purpose and goals saying, "*The common enemy of humanity is man. In searching for a new enemy to unite us, we came up with the idea that pollution, the threat of global warming, water shortages, famine and the like would fit the bill. All of these dangers are caused by human intervention, and it is only through changed attitudes and behavior that they can be overcome. The real enemy then, is humanity itself."*

Diabolical! Turn man against himself so that every aspect of human life is a threat. In order to subjugate the entire human race, get man to imprison himself. First to be targeted, of course, would have to be the three pillars of freedom: free enterprise, individuality and private property.

What is this new diabolical tool that now leads the forces of global control over all humanity and which is quickly invading every single level of our government, our communities, and our neighborhoods? Its name is Sustainable Development.

THE COMPREHENSIVE BLUEPRINT

After decades of planning and sponsoring international gatherings to lay the groundwork for the plan, finally all was ready. So in 1992, the United Nations presented a new document to the world. It was called the "Comprehensive Blueprint" for the reorganization of human society. The reason the reorganization was necessary, according to the UN, was that the Earth was in crisis because of mankind's disregard for the environment – right out of the Club of Rome's playbook. Therefore, of course, the world was in crisis and drastic action had to be taken to save it. The plan was named the Agenda for the 21st Century - or simply Agenda 21.

The preamble to the Agenda 21 document said: *"Humanity stands at a defining moment in history. We are confronted with a perpetuation of disparities between and within nations, a worsening of poverty, hunger, ill health and illiteracy, and the continuing deterioration of the ecosystem on which we depend for our well-being. However, integration of environment and development concerns and greater attention to them will lead to the fulfillment of basic needs, improved living standards for all, better protected and managed ecosystems and a safer, more prosperous future. No nation can achieve this on its own; but together we can – in a global partnership for sustainable development."*

The document went on to say: *"Effective execution of Agenda 21 will require a profound reorientation of all human society, unlike anything the world has ever experienced. A major shift in the priorities of both governments and individuals and an unprecedented redeployment of human and financial resources; this shift will demand that a concern for the environmental consequences of every human action be integrated into individual and collective decision-making at every level."*

Agenda 21 held all of the tenets of the socialist promise of a better, safer, fulfilled future, if only people would surrender to the common good offered by the grand plan. Fear is always the most effective tool in establishing power, and so the grand plan to reorganize the entire human society was launched.

However, if the plan is to grab power globally, then it is vital to eliminate any source of independent resistance. First step, eliminate the concept of independent sovereign nations. The UN's Commission on Global Governance launched that effort saying: "*The concept of national sovereignty has been immutable, indeed a sacred principle of international relations. It is a principle which will yield only slowly and reluctantly to the new imperatives of global environmental cooperation.*" Their argument is that independent nations are the root of wars, strife, competition and poverty.

The second step was the establishment of the need to roll back the concepts of debate and difference of opinion. The vote of the people through a ballot box was not a consideration since we faced a crisis created by those very voters. To that purpose, again, the Club of Rome issued this statement: "*Democracy is not a panacea. It cannot organize everything and it is unaware of its own limitations. These facts must be faced squarely. Sacrilegious though it may sound, democracy is no longer well suited for the tasks at hand. The complexity and the technical nature of many of today's problems do not always allow elected representatives to make competent decisions at the right time.*" In other words, a dictatorship is much more effective than letting silly individuals make decisions for themselves.

Yet, as these grand schemes were promoted on the international scene, one major obstacle remained: the United States, the one nation built on the pillars of freedom, including free enterprise, private property, individuality, independence, and national sovereignty. If ever this new force for global power was going to gain full control, it had to find a way to deal with the United States and its infernal ideas of freedom. But how could they get Americans to surrender their entire history and culture?

Begin by attacking the governing documents that promote and permit such ideas. To change those attitudes, it's vital to get Americans to question the validity of their very foundation.

The attack on our founding documents has been on-going for several decades, through control of the public education system, the news media, and political debate. As a result, there is no doubt that the people of the United States today are deeply divided in their ideas and philosophy about the proper role of government. There are certainly those who revere the Constitution as the greatest governing document in history; they argue that it simply needs to be adhered to in order to preserve individual liberty.

Others have been influenced to see the Constitution as a "living document" open to interpretation "to respond to our changing times and changing moral values." The flood gates were opened to the central argument for changing our American system of government by such advocates as futurist Amitai Etzioni who said, ". . . we are not irrevocably bound by what was written two hundred years ago."

This idea is the main tool used by those who seek to change the United States, and to "harmonize" it to fit in with the rest of the world. It suggests that the Founders couldn't possibly have foreseen our modern world with its complex problems. That argument is the very crack in the foundation that is leading to the coming flood of change that will lead us to tyranny.

Consider the use of the terms "our changing moral values", and "we are not irrevocably bound by what was written two hundred years ago." In order to move from Locke's ideas of individual rights and freedom into socialism/communism, a central state must serve as a coordinating agency. Most consider that central state to be the United Nations, as many look upon it to be the great moral leader for a changing human society. Of course, the UN's interpretation of morality is far different from that of Locke's. When the definition of morality becomes fluid to meet the need of the State to reinvent society, an entire culture and its founding ideas are replaced and forgotten. Ideas such as property ownership and individual liberties become old fashioned and out of date.

The Founders' intended restraints on those who might seek to use government to enforce their ideas are in the way of global control. Now considered out of date, they must be removed from policy making. Thus the snide argument was born that, "well, the founders were intelligent guys, but come on, how could they foresee such problems as energy shortages or traffic jams?" Such simple arguments have now worked on an increasingly forgetful, uninformed and misled citizenry.

Consequently, that cultural change has become entrenched in U.S. public policy, just as the power-mongers had planned. We are witnessing the very transformation of a nation that once prospered on the ideas of free enterprise, individualism, and private property ownership – all to be removed and replaced with a new concept for human governance.

Using the claim of the Constitution as a "living document," proponents have successfully opened the United States into accepting the concept of global harmony with the grand plans of worldwide Sustainable Development.

Finally, the full goal of the plan was revealed by none other than the former head of the communist Soviet Union, Mikhail Gorbachev when he addressed the State of the World Forum: "*The emerging 'environmentalization' of our civilization and the need for vigorous action in the interest of the entire global community will inevitably have multiple political consequences. Perhaps the most important of them will be a gradual change in the status of the United Nations. **Inevitably, it must assume some aspects of world government.**"*

How do forces who are determined to rule the world do it without firing a shot while, indeed, gaining the voluntary help of the victims they intend to conquer? No stone has been left unturned. Under the banner of Sustainable Development they have worked their way into every level of government and its agencies, educational institutions, major corporations, the news media, entertainment, social media, and every part of society's discourse of ideas.

The mantra of conquest is heard throughout the world, "If we are to save the planet – the forces to save 'Mother Earth' must move forward in a three pronged attack: eliminate free enterprise, replace the individual with the community, and remove all aspects of private property for the common good and social justice." To oppose this powerful force is to bring massive condemnation, threatening the very concepts of political debate and free speech, not to mention the entire field of scientific research. Napoleon, Hitler and Stalin would have been in awe.

CHAPTER FIVE

"SUSTAINABLE DEVELOPMENT" THE CODE WORD FOR REORGANIZATION

It's in every city in the nation. You hear it talked about in city council meetings and state legislatures. It's sold as the bold visionary plan for our future. But is it? Or is Sustainable Development the answer for the complete reorganization of human society as called for in Agenda 21?

We are assured by local officials and planners that Sustainable Development is simply a tool or a guideline to help guide the carefully-planned growth of our cities and rural areas while protecting our natural resources for future generations. Proponents sell the concept of Sustainable Development through familiar, unthreatening words and beautiful pictures.

ILLUSTRATION BY PETE ELLIS/DRAWGOOD.COM

Take a close look at the graphic posted above. It's from Nature magazine. The publication used this image to accompany an article about the glories of Sustainable Development. It depicts an individual who is trying to decide on the proper road to take. The road leading to the left heads toward an ugly, gray city with belching smoke stacks. It is clearly marked "Economic Growth." The other road, leading to the right, heads toward a beautiful rural landscape of tall trees and lush green grass. It is boldly marked "Sustainable Progress."

Which do we choose? The chaos of the capitalist's industrial revolution that brought us pollution and the destruction of the planet? Or do we choose peace, serenity and calm, living as one with nature?

What is missing in the graphic when the road is taken toward the obviously positive, utopian depiction of Sustainable progress? There are no homes, no jobs, and no human activity. In reality, the description in the graphic is an honest representation of the true purpose of Sustainable Development: free enterprise eliminated, individualism vastly reduced along with massive numbers of the population; and no private property to be fenced in and locked away for personal use. This they call utopia!

Based on stacks of policy statements, documents, and speeches from a wide variety of national and international gatherings, proponents reveal their belief that the free enterprise system upsets their vision of a well-ordered society. They claim that a free-market system that has no controls on development, creates jobs, private housing, and luxury beyond mere human existence levels, is dangerous because we don't know where it might lead.

If that sounds difficult to accept, consider these facts. In 2012, the United Nations held an event to celebrate twenty years since the introduction of Agenda 21. At this 20th anniversary event, called Rio+20, several speakers expanded on the vision of Agenda 21, promoting a concept called "Zero Economic Growth" as the means to preserve the planet and its resources. The idea suggests zero factories, zero housing growth, and zero human activity. Look again at the graphic above. Does the description of Zero Economic Growth fit perfectly in the concept that *Nature* is promoting? It clearly says that economic growth – human activity – means belching smokes stacks and environmental destruction?

Such images, constantly depicted, eventually begin to take their toll as they convince the American people to sacrifice freedom of choice and, instead, accept systematic, top-down control over our society. Essentially this graphic and many more like it, as regularly seen on television, in magazines, children's textbooks, and in government public meetings, are carefully designed to create an instant Pavlovian knee-jerk reaction to any proposals offered contrary to the Sustainable agenda. People are being carefully conditioned so that, when the environment is mentioned, their eyes glaze over in automatic acceptance and the ability to reason or question simply shuts down.

Do you not believe that is true? Here's a test for you. Ask your school-aged child a question about the environment and listen to his or her description of the coming destruction of the Earth, resulting because of man's selfish grab for material comforts. Then offer a contrary viewpoint, perhaps suggesting that such ideas have no strong basis in science. Watch their eyes. Witness their frustration as they try to consider a comeback. Now see them push that idea away, again focusing on the coming destruction of the Earth. It is nearly guaranteed that the discussion will make little progress from that point. As Pavlov did with his research dogs, give your child a dog biscuit and pat them on the head for they have responded properly to their training.

The scary part is that you will get the identical reaction to your questions at the local planning meeting with your city council members. Try to oppose Sustainable policy projects by discussing private property protection, individual choice, or free enterprise…worse yet, just say the words Agenda 21 and you will get a roll of the eyes and a deep sigh as they dismiss anything you have to say. Knick Knack, Patty Whack, give your councilman a dog biscuit. The behavior modification serves the cause yet again.

Once more the global forces who seek to transform and control our society have scored a victory. You've heard it said that our children are our future. To assure that is true, the global forces are busy perfecting them to be the perfect global village citizens.

Sustainable Development is the code word for that future village. What will it be like living in that sustainable village?

WHAT IS SUSTAINABLE DEVELOPMENT?

Most people immediately equate Sustainable Development with environmental policy. Of course, concern for the environment is the justification most often given for the implementation of Sustainable Development. Land use control is at the heart of Sustainable Development policy, but assuming it is simply good environmental stewardship proves to be a serious and dangerous mistake.

The term "Sustainable Development" was born in the pages of "Our Common Future," the official report of the 1987 United Nations World Commission on Environment and Development, authored by Gro Harlem Brundtland, Vice President of the World Socialist Party. Since its publication the world has never been the same.

Sustainable Development appeared in full force in Agenda 21. As given by its proponents, the most common definition of Sustainable Development is: "*Development that meets the needs of the present without compromising the ability of future generations to meet their own needs.*" Again this simple-worded, positive-sounding definition hides an agenda that can only lead to a breathtaking transformation of society and top-down control over human progress by a select few.

According to its advocates, to achieve the goal of meeting today's needs without compromising the needs of the future requires massive amounts of land and natural resources to be permanently locked away from use; that means control, not conservation. More importantly, according to them, it requires an entirely new way of thinking about how society is to be organized.

In order to fully comprehend the magnitude of the changes required to enforce Sustainable Development, a much more descriptive and honest definition is necessary. After years of studying the subject, this is mine: *Imagine an America in which a specific "ruling principle" is created to decide proper societal conduct for every citizen. That principle would be used to determine regulations guiding everything you eat, the size of home you are allowed, the method of transportation you use to get to work, what kind of work you may have, the way you dispose of waste, perhaps even the number of children you may have, as well as the quality and amount of education your children may receive.* Again, Sustainable Development encompasses every aspect of our lives.

In short, Sustainable Development requires a complete transformation of American society including our system of justice, our economic system, and our ability to make individual life choices such as careers, family size, and the location of our homes. This is the "wrenching transformation of society" Al Gore was talking about in his book, *Earth in the Balance.* He claims this radical reorganization of human existence on earth is necessary in order to cleanse our society of the purported evils of the 20th Century's Industrial Revolution.

Those are pretty powerful words that should concern anyone trying to make their way in our modern world. It's a warning that the rules are changing and that a new power elite is taking control.

Perhaps you are beginning to notice such changes as you go about your daily routine – but haven't understood from where those changes are coming, and the ideas behind them. There are Sustainable Development papers, guidelines and regulations to impose the ruling principle:

» On our **public education system** – to prepare our children to be proper "global citizens" living in a sustainable world. Today that curriculum is called Common Core. In the classrooms, assuring the children have the proper global attitudes, values, and beliefs is much more important than teaching basic academics. Behavior modification is the real curriculum of today's public education system. "Globally-Acceptable Truth" is an actual UN concept that dictates the science and knowledge we are allowed to pursue. It says the reason we have wars, strife and poverty is because there is too much knowledge that makes it hard for people to know how to make the right decisions. So government will allow us only that knowledge which will promote sustainability and they will make all decisions for us to provide their definition of a happier, healthier, stress-free life. This concept is now the root of the public education system. The result can only be a population with limited knowledge and skills, yet unquestioning of authority and easily pliable to fulfill specific, mindless tasks to serve the collective. The systematic production of Global Village Idiots unable to question authority is the result.

» On our **economy** – the focus has become the creation of public/private partnerships (PPPs) between business and government. Business becomes a tool for implementing government policies while government moves quietly behind the supposed independence of business. In this way government power grows while hiding behind a smokescreen that may look like a free market of independent choice. It's not. Corporations that play ball get extra benefits like tax breaks and more desirable locations in the development of the community, as they go to the head of the line for project approval. In this way they are able to use the power of government to help put their competition out of business. That's not free enterprise.

» On the **environment** – controls on personal use of private property and business decisions, including products to be produced and the materials to produce them. Under Sustainable Development, environmental protection becomes the excuse for all policy decisions, regardless of whether the environment would even be affected. It's called the "precautionary principle." It forces long delays and massive studies over what might, could, maybe happen if all the stars are properly aligned with the moon on any given day of the week before deciding if a policy or business plan is a danger to the environment. In short, the precautionary principle is a killer of economies – especially when the final decision is being made by boards and panels and councils armed with a very specific anti-business bias.

» On **healthcare** – Just as Sustainable Development is a private property land grab, Sustainable Medicine is a body grab. One of its promises for a "healthy community" is an environment free of too many people. The current debate on the existence of "rationed" health care is right out of the Sustainable playbook as it considers older people and the sick to be no longer valuable resources to society, in their words, useless eaters. Simply do a Google search for "sustainable medicine" to fine more than five million references, including most of the details that were eventually included in the Affordable Care Act.

» On **farming** – Sustainable Development policies affect farmers' ability to produce more crops by regulating necessary chemicals, energy, and water use in the name of environmental protection. Non-Governmental Organizations (NGOs) and environmental groups, working hand-in-hand with government agencies, seek to control the means of production of food consumed by the American people. In the name of "social justice" all food production, distribution and consumption would be controlled by government. Shortages and hunger can be the only logical result. To fully understand the folly of sustainable farming, one should take a good look at current agriculture courses in several colleges (check out Green Mountain College in Vermont) and agriculture symposiums that now feature the use of oxen as replacements for non-sustainable gas-guzzling tractors. Students are paying for a college education to learn Davy Crockett's farming methods. Need more be said? Sustainable farming forces up the cost of producing crops. Small, independent farmers cannot compete. Sustainable farming benefits only large corporate farms – again Public/Private Partnerships (PPPs). If small, independent farmers have signed Conservation Easements and sold their development rights, eventually they may lose their farms and then the property goes to land trusts, and is eventually locked away from production forever.

» On our **social and cultural environment** – political correctness is a vital tool for the creation of an automatic response to a given situation eliminating the requirement to think and fully analyze an issue. As a result, few ever need to question the enforcement of policies that endanger national sovereignty and eliminate our historic culture. "It's for the environment." 'It isn't fair to stop the migration of people from one place to another." "Racist." "I don't want to hear your mean comments. It makes me uncomfortable." "I'm offended."

» On our **mobility** – with emphasis on carpools and public transportation. $4 per gallon of gas is purely Sustainable Development policies in action, designed to ban drilling of more oil, specifically American oil, in order to create shortages and drive up the price to get us out of our cars and into public transportation. The latest development in controlling freedom of movement is the creation of driverless cars pre-programmed to their destination in stacked and packed high-rise mega cities.

» And on **public safety** – the rule of law and the court system is being challenged by new laws and regulations that affect the right to privacy and unreasonable search and seizures. According to Sustainable doctrine, the REAL ID Act and the creation of a total surveillance society -- using biometrics to track our every move will insure we are being properly sustainable in our daily lives. Cars are being taxed on the number of miles driven. As populations grow in the mega Smart Growth cities, violence, too, grows. Cameras on every corner monitor our every move. Smart meters are being forced on private homes to control energy use. New appliances are being manufactured to talk to the meters in order to fully unify every electrical unit in the home without human interference. The excuse for all of it is cutting our carbon footprint for the safety and protection of the environment. The result is control.

It is essential that every American understands that these leading issues we face today are not just random concerns that accidentally find their way into the forefront of political debate. They are all interconnected to the policies of Sustainable Development and the restructuring of our way of life.

CHAPTER SIX

HOW TO MAKE IT "LAW OF THE LAND"

Proponents of Agenda 21 argue that it is not a treaty and has no enforcement power, thus it is not a threat, just a suggestion of ideas for future planning. It is true that it's not a treaty. Rather Agenda 21 is known as "soft-law," meaning it is basically suggested policy. So how did it become a threat, enforced in every community in the nation?

Agenda 21 was written and prepared for the Earth Summit by hundreds of private, non-governmental organizations (NGOs) working inside the UN structure. Each NGO has its own private agenda that it connived to have included in the final version of Agenda 21. Once 179 heads of state, including U.S. President George H.W. Bush, signed the document in a ceremony at the Earth Summit, the NGOs headed into those governments to help them implement the *Earth Summit/ Agenda 21* blue print into official policy.

In 1993, President Bill Clinton, in order to impose Agenda 21 policy, created the President's Council on Sustainable Development (PCSD). Members of the same NGO groups that wrote Agenda 21 were now part of the PCSD, including the Sierra Club, Nature Conservancy, and the National Wildlife Federation, to name a few. These NGOs helped write major grant programs for the EPA, HUD, and other federal agencies. The grant programs included specific requirements that directly complied to Agenda 21-defined Sustainable policies. In accepting the grants, communities agreed to implement those plans.

The PCSD then issued a comprehensive report containing all the guidelines on how our government was to be reinvented under Sustainable Development. It involved nearly every agency of the federal government. It was the President's Council that turned Agenda 21 from "suggested" policy to policy enforceable by law and affecting every single federal agency, state government, and local community government.

Yet the policies are written using less-than-direct language, leaving them to interpretation by the agencies. While it sounds reasonable and non-threatening on the surface, one has the feeling something import-ant is missing. The concept seems complicated for the average person to grasp, making it difficult to argue against. That is unless one understands the full agenda behind the purpose of Sustainable Development.

Here is the official description of Sustainable Development issued by the Presidents Council on Sustainable Development:

"Sustainable Communities encourage people to work together to create healthy communities where natural resources and historic resources are preserved, jobs are available, sprawl is contained, neighborhoods are secure, education is lifelong, transportation and health care are accessible, and all citizens have opportunities to improve the quality of their lives."

Notice the language used – carefully selected to sound positive, paint-ing images of stability and normalcy. Jobs. Education. History. Health. Opportunity. All the things needed for a stable, happy community. Nothing to argue about. Nothing to fear. However, to fully understand the meaning of that statement and its consequences on our traditional American system, one must break down the language and ask key ques-tions. To ask the right questions, of course, requires us to understand the real goal in the process and the tactics being used to achieve it.

In 1966, without ever having heard the term Sustainable Develop-ment or read its policies, historian Jo Hindman's discerning knowledge of totalitarian policy understood exactly what government agencies at every level would need to do to violate traditional, accepted, legal protec-tions of private property in order to enforce the ravages of this top-down control: *"The strategy is to make property ownership so unbearable by harassment through building inspections, remodeling orders, fines and jail-ings, that owners give up in despair and sell to land developers at cut-rate prices. Punitive municipal codes are the weapons in the warfare."* These are exactly the policies and tactics used today in every single community, state and federal agency to impose Sustainable Develpment.

It's interesting to note that in 1968, a Soviet Russian architect, named Alexei Gutnov, wrote a book outlining the details for the creation of perfect utopian cities in order to integrate Communist philosophy into the everyday lives of the citizens. The book was authorized by the Soviet government through the University of Moscow's architecture faculty. In particular, the plan was to control, not only where the people lived, but also how they lived. The book is titled *The Ideal Communist City.*

According to the book "*The chaotic growth of cities will be replaced by a dynamic system of urban settlement,*" Gutnov goes on to describe the creations of zones or regions to oversee and control every inch of living space, commerce and industry placement. "*The region is formed by the economic interdependence of its development, from the industrial complex to the industrial area and industrial region. The region has a single system of transportation, a centralized administration, and a united system of education and research.*"

There you have it. *The Ideal Communist City.* Is it a coincidence that it is also the nearly identical description used by planners in creating "local" Sustainable Development programs? You will find some of the exact language used by planning groups in describing the reasons for their plans and their goals. "Chaotic growth" must be controlled. Light-rail trains will interconnect cities in the region. "Centralized Administration" of the process. Education is life-long.

Could it be that Sustainable Development really is an extension of the master plan for the ideal communist city? Of course, when selling the concept to local governments on their redevelopment plans, proponents of Sustainable Development deny it. However, a closer look at things they do say to each other in unguarded moments, tell a very different story.

Here are just a few of the statements Sustainable Development proponents have actually said in truly describing their intentions. These are rarely mentioned in the news media or in polite company. But they said these things, nonetheless.

"*Land… cannot be treated as an ordinary asset, controlled by individuals and subject to the pressures and inefficiencies of the market. Private land ownership is also a principle instrument of accumulation and concentration of wealth, therefore contributes to social injustice.*" **Report from UN's Habitat 1 Conference, 1976.**

"*We reject the idea of private property.*" **Peter Berle, National Audubon Society**

"*(We) will map the whole nation…determine development for the whole country, and regulate it all…*" **Thomas Lovejoy (Science Advisor to the Department of Interior)**

"*Individual rights will have to take a back seat to the collective.*" **Harvey Ruvin (Vice Chairman, ICLEI)**

"*What then is the most effective transition strategy? The essential aim is not to fight against consumer - capitalist society, but to build the alternative to it.*" **Author Ted Trainer, Transition to a Sustainable and Just World.**

"*It doesn't matter what is true. It only matters what people believe is true.*" **Paul Watson (co-founder of Greenpeace.)**

"*This is the first time in the history of mankind that we are setting ourselves the task of intentionally, within a defined period of time, to change the economic development model that has been reigning for at least 150 years, since the industrial revolution...*"

Christiana Figueres (Executive Secretary, UN Framework Convention on Climate Change)

These are the real goals of Sustainable Development, revealed in the global warriors' own words. They openly attack free enterprise, individualism and private property rights. And these are the goals of their entrenched eco-warriors now operating in nearly every federal and state agency and every city planning department in the nation. If this coordinated assault is successful, the United States of America and its founding Constitution cannot survive.

How do they enforce these ideas? They organize a massive system of programs, rules and regulations, steadily promoted by representatives of thousands of NGO organizations, planning groups, and government agents, all operating in the background of your local governments. Once eyes have been opened, it's much easier to see it in action, right in ones own back yard.

CHAPTER SEVEN

SETTING THE STAGE
HOW TO SELL THE GLOBAL PLAN

Never in the history of human society has there been a more complete, comprehensive, top-down plan to transform and control the world as is taking place under the banner of Sustainable Development. It appeals to the masses, claiming the righteousness of "international interdependence." "We're all in this together" is the hard-to-resist battle cry. Let's all join together in a group hug! And the world voluntarily joins in to accept "living on less for the greater good." Few ask if it is necessary or reasonable. Fewer still ask who or what is the greater good. The goals of Sustainable Development are rarely specific, usually relying on relative generalities that are hard to pin down or research. The precept that "everyone knows…" seems to work for most.

Obviously it takes careful planning, a massive organization, political power and lots of access to large amounts of cash. Those behind the Sustainable movement have plenty of it all. They have used their assets wisely, always with their eye on the goal. Carefully the power elite have covered every facet of our society to bring it all in line with the "new think" for their brave new world. The goal is achieved by carefully controlling thoughts, actions, income generation, and the marketplace. In short, their every move is designed to eliminate free enterprise, individuality, and private property.

The depth and forethought of their execution of the plan is massive. It seems nothing is left to chance:

» **Control the Marketplace.** One would assume that the greatest enemy for their proposed planned economy would be business. They have conquered that. Today, major corporations use their product development and huge advertising budgets to spread the propaganda of the necessity for environmentally-correct sustainable products. Never mind that such products cost the consumer more as these policies damage competition that isn't "in the game." The companies get rewards and plaques for their efforts. Hotels place instructions in their rooms reminding us to reuse towels and sheets – in order to save the environment. In reality these "environmentally correct" policies save the companies money and increase profits as they get us to voluntarily accept less service with no discount in price. Clever twist! The message to companies – Play ball and get the rewards! How better to control that infernal capitalism than to dangle higher profits in front of them. Of course, to play in such a game you've just killed the competition of a true free market. It's all for the common good! Mission accomplished.

» **Private property means** our homes. They have us voluntarily accepting controls, and even anxious to sacrifice our back yards for the pleasure of a small balcony in a crowded high rise. Large homes have become environmentally incorrect – scoffed at as "McMansions." Such homes used to be the desirable dream. A place in the suburbs with room for the kids to play and the family to grow. To make them undesirable it just takes constant rate hikes in utilities and property taxes. And of course there is that never ending drumbeat of environmental protection, warning that those awful suburbs ("urban sprawl") are taking the habitat away from the poor animals. The promise of happy, healthy neighborhoods in the cities has become a call for people to rush to the cities to live in the ever-smaller condos with their plants on the balconies. Of course, there's a park down the street so the kids can touch the ground once in a while. The dream of private property becomes a thing from a less enlightened era. Mission Accomplished.

» **Eliminate Cars.** The best example of America's love affair with independence is expressed in our devotion to our cars…our private, personal source of transportation. We can go as we choose without worrying about meeting someone else's schedule. And our cars will take us straight to our destination. It's the ultimate freedom. Yet they've managed to make the pumping of a bicycle uphill seem more appealing. The assault on private transportation comes through a vast number of well thought out schemes. First, as the free-market has managed to actually lower the cost of gasoline, clever politicians see a chance to void that reduction by putting in new taxes at the pump. So the auto owner doesn't benefit – the state does. Keep the prices of fuel high and people will drive less. Next, tax the number of miles the car is driven each year. It's now being done. Don't build new roads so the existing ones become more crowded and commutes to work become unbearable. Then, of course there is old faithful – make the cars share the road with bikes. There's nothing more exciting than trying to get through crowded streets while following some guy pumping as fast as he can. And when you finally get home to your high-rise condo you realize that adding parking lots is taboo, so now there is nowhere to put the car. You finally give in, get rid of the car, and take the bus. Mission Accomplished.

» **Lock away the land.** Those who love the great outdoors, hiking, climbing, and recreational vehicles have been recruited to promote the Sustainable agenda, even though it leads to blocking human activity from vast amounts of the great outdoors. As more land is locked away, through the establishment of national monuments, heritage areas, parks, and so on, those who claim a love for the great outdoors believe they now have new places to explore. However, in many cases they are shocked to find that is not true. "No Trespassing" signs are erected. Human activity is banned. No boating on the river. No hiking in the foothills. The excuse? Man drags in invasive species. Remember the warning from the Club of Rome -- man is the enemy, the environment is not for his use. There are great efforts made to keep man out of the environment and safely locked away in the cities where he belongs. One such program is called the Wildlands Project which calls for locking away 50% of all the land in the United States. The goal is to keep man out of the wilderness in the name of environmental protection. Mission Accomplished.

» **Eliminate local Control.** Do you believe in small government and local control? The planners for Sustainable Development will convince you that they do too! They will assure you that all of their plans are just local ideas created by the input of local citizens. Funny thing, though… do a simple Google search for Sustainable Development and you will find the exact same plans with nearly identical language for communities and nations all over the world. Usually the plans end in numbers like 2030 or 2050. You'll find plans like Jamaica 2050 or Dubai 2050. These are almost identical with plans in the United States like Heartland 2050, covering multiple counties around Omaha, or Virginia Beach 2040. If you look closely enough you'll find the exact same language in all of them. One thing they all have in common is that none are local; more often than not, the same planning "experts" are brought in from across the nation to write the plan. Sustainable Development is a global plan to reorganize human society under a one-size-fits-all scheme. Every single state and community in the United States is now implementing major parts of this identical plan. Mission Accomplished.

» **Erase history.** Is the history of the nation a passion for you? Do you love learning about our past, how we developed, perhaps you enjoy visiting historic sites like Presidential birthplaces? You want to make sure that the battlefield where they fought, and the neighborhoods where they walked are preserved. It's called our heritage. Of course your studies of the ideals of the Founders have led you to share their passion for keeping government under control. There's no way you would support a global plan to rule the world through the United Nations. You are, and should be, the greatest threat to the implementation of Sustainable Development policies. No way will they get your support! Wanna bet? The Sustainablists know all about you and the threat you pose to their plans. So they have prepared special programs to reel you in. One is called Historic Preservation. The plan is to simply lock away every inch of ground historic figures ever walked on – just to honor them, of course. There's historic preservation of downtown areas in nearly every city – even where nothing historic ever happened. Funded by grant money the Sustainablists use the preservation excuse to deny private property rights to owners, keeping them from making any changes on buildings. Of course, if they want to make changes to an area of downtown they just use eminent domain and a bulldozer. Battlefield preservation means massive amounts of land locked away, including land that wasn't part of the battle. Gettysburg, Pennsylvania is a prime example. The actual battlefield was originally mapped out by the soldiers who fought there. It has been well preserved for over 100 years. But today the community's natural growth, local businesses and private property have been stunted by control of the National Park Service. Via a ban on growth, Gettysburg is forever trapped in July, 1863. Mission Accomplished.

How do they sell such ideas that entrap whole communities, property owners, businesses, city councils, county commissions, entire populations, and even opponents to accept an ever-growing monster of uncontrolled government?

There are a near endless list of programs and tools to make it happen. A new language has been invented for government. Attend any city council or county commission meeting and you'll hear this new language used routinely. Where once city councils conducted their business concerning the paving of streets, storm sewer improvements, or welcoming new business into town, today such city business seems quant and unimportant.

City Councils today have much more important, loftier goals to discuss. The new language includes discussions of: Wetlands, conservation easements, watersheds, viewsheds, rails–to-trails programs, biosphere reserves, greenways, reducing our carbon footprints, partnerships with business, preservation, stakeholder councils, land use, environmental protection, development, diversity, visioning, open space, heritage areas, and comprehensive planning. These items are all part of the new language of government. Each one of these items leads to controls, outright banning of products, shortages, higher consumer costs, and, ultimately, bigger government.

The little known side effect of such programs is a forced sacrifice by the citizens as each program affects their property, pocketbooks and quality of life. But hey, it's just the way government is done now– don't you know?

To make sure these policies aren't opposed -- and in fact have the appearance of public acceptance, a clever, yet cynical new tactic is often used for public meetings. The reality is that, using this tactic, the programs are presented in a manner that convinces the people of the community that all of the ideas were their own. Private NGO groups, planners, government agents and community leaders you've probably never heard of are actually running these meetings. The people of the community are told they need to accept these ideas because these leaders are experts, and have titles! We are assured that these experts who are using terms you've never heard before, are obviously the ones in the know – and we are not!

Consensus is the new god of government. It's a pre-determined outcome. A professional facilitator is employed to lead the meeting to assure that pre-determined outcome is achieved. Forget Roberts Rules of Order where everyone has a chance to speak for and against. Even though perhaps only ten people show up for the meeting (and nine of those ten are the planners and NGOs), if all agree to the program (and they will) – that's consensus – local approval for our local plan. There have also been cases where opposition did show up and express its disapproval. Regardless the protests were ignored and the plan moved forward anyway. Those who disagree are usually singled-out for ridicule in front of the gathering. With such intimidation tactics employed by professionals, who would dare question the outcome? The official interpretation becomes the party line - that the community has spoken. We have taken direct action for our future!

Welcome to the brave new world of Sustainable Development and the transformation of America. This is how it's done. The process moves forward in a two-pronged attack. Specific programs are devised for the rural areas of the nation; another set of plans focus on the cities. In the rural areas it's called the Wildlands Project. In the cities it's called Smart Growth. From these two approaches a wide array of programs, regulations and grant programs have been devised, and each comes with its own army of NGOs and planners to force them into place. The goal for both is the complete implementation of Agenda 21/Sustainable Development.

The forces behind it are patient, amazingly thorough, and organized to assure the entire plan is completed, down to the tiniest details of changing the attitudes, values and beliefs of the nation -- resulting in changing our entire culture and system of government; **in short, the complete transformation of human society.**

CHAPTER EIGHT

ATTACK OF THE NGOS

WARNING!

This chapter uses a whole lot of letters and abbreviations because government loves Acronyms. To help the reader keep them all straight, here is a reference list: These are just a few of the thousands of organizations, agencies, and, interested players working together to enforce Sustainable Development on our entire world.

(The Head of the Monster)
United Nations: UN
(The Matrix Control Center)
United Nations Environmental Program: UNEP
(The Big Three)
World Wide Fund for Nature: WWF
World Resources Institute: WRI
International Union of Conservation and Nature: IUCN
(The Ground Troops)
Non-governmental Organizations: NGOs
(Source of the Plan)
United Nations Conference on Environment and Development: UNCED
(US Government Forces)
Environmental Protection Agency: EPA
United States Forest Service: USFS
National Park Service: NPS
(Useful Idiots)
American Planning Association: APA
Piedmont Environmental Council: PEC
(Every community has its own local version of this one)

One rarely hears of it. Few elected officials raise an eyebrow. The media makes no mention of it. Yet, power is slowly slipping away from our locally-elected representatives into the hands of private, non–elected people and organizations. They come equipped with their own agenda, enforced by thousands of dedicated activists – and armed with a bunch of money. In much the same way Mao Tse-tung had his Red Guards, so the forces for global transformation have their NGOs. They may well be our masters tomorrow, yet most people don't even know who or what they are.

There are, in fact, two parallel, complimentary forces operating in the world, working together to advance the global Sustainable Development agenda, ultimately driving toward UN controlled global governance. Those two forces are the UN itself and its affiliated non-governmental organizations (NGO).

Beginning with the United Nations, the infrastructure pushing the Sustainable Development agenda is a vast, international matrix. At the top of the heap is the United Nations Environmental Program (UNEP). Created in 1973 by the UN General Assembly, the UNEP is the catalyst through which the global environmental agenda is implemented. Virtually all of the international environmental programs and policy changes that have occurred globally, over the past four decades, are the result of UNEP efforts.

But the UNEP doesn't operate on its own. Influencing it and helping to write policy are thousands of non-governmental organizations (NGOs). These are private groups, each of which, seeks to implement a specific political agenda according to its own charter. There are hundreds of these groups covering every issue of Sustainable Development. NGOs are also referred to as "Civil Society" in UN documents. A quick look at local government planning policies will see them referred to as "Stakeholders" for the community, even though they are seldom from that area. Through the UN infrastructure, particularly through the UNEP, they have great power.

The phrase "non-governmental organization" came into use with the establishment of the United Nations Organization in 1945 with provisions in Article 71 of Chapter 10 of the United Nations Charter. The term describes a consultative role for organizations that are neither government nor member states of the UN.

OFFICIAL UN RECOGNITION OF NGOS (FROM THE UN CHARTER)

The Economic and Social Council may make suitable arrangements for consultation with non-governmental organizations which are concerned with matters within its competence. Such arrangements may be made with international organizations and where appropriate, with national organizations after consultation with the Member of the United Nations concerned."

An NGO is not just any private group hoping to influence policy. True NGOs are officially sanctioned by the United Nations. Such status was created by UN Resolution #1296 in 1948, giving NGOs official "Consultative" status to the UN. That means they not only can sit in on international meetings, but can actively participate in creating policy, right along side government representatives and diplomats.

OFFICIAL RULES TO BE AN OFFICIAL UNITED NATIONS NGO

Principles to be Applied in the Establishment of Consultative Relations
The following principles shall be applied in establishing consultative relations with non-governmental organizations:

1. The organization shall be concerned with matters falling within the competence of the Economic and Social Council with respect to international economic, social, cultural, educational, health, scientific, technological and related matters and to questions of human rights.
2. The aims and purposes of the organization shall be in conformity with the spirit, purposes and principles of the Charter of the United Nations.
3. The organization shall undertake to support the work of the United Nations and to promote knowledge of its principles and activities, in accordance with its own aims and purposes and the nature and scope of its competence and activities.

There are numerous classifications of NGOs. The two most common are "Operational" and "Advocacy."

Operational NGOs are involved with designing and implementing specific projects such as feeding the hungry or organizing relief projects. These groups can be religious or secular. They can be community-based, national, or international. The International Red Cross falls under the category of an operational NGO.

Advocacy NGOs are promoting specific political agendas. They lobby government bodies, use the news media, and organize activist-oriented events, all designed to raise awareness and apply pressure to promote their causes which include environmental issues, human rights, poverty, education, children, drinking water, and population control -- to name just a few.

Amnesty International is the largest human rights advocacy NGO in the world. Organized globally, it has more than 1.8 million members, supporters, and subscribers in over 150 countries.

Today these NGOs have power nearly equal to member nations when it comes to writing UN policy. Just as civil service bureaucrats provide the infrastructure for government operation, NGOs provide such infrastructure for the UN In fact, most UN policy is first debated and then written by the NGOs and presented to national government officials at international meetings for approval and ratification. It is through this process that the individual political agendas of the NGO groups enter the international political arena.

The policies sometimes come in the form of international treaties, others are offered simply as policy guidelines. Once the documents are presented and accepted by representatives of member states and world leaders, obscure political agendas of private organizations suddenly become international policy. **They are then adopted as national and local laws by UN member nations**, with no treaty necessary to be authorized by Congress. Along with the NGOs and national government representatives, the UN's web includes representatives from international corporations, academia, and journalists. It's a near total web of control in all aspects of our lives.

The funding for these activities comes from a wide array of government program and from private foundations such as the Ford Foundation, the Rockefeller Foundation, McArthur Foundation, and many more such foundations, and, of course George Soros. NGO groups working on environmental issues have a near limitless source of funds from the

Environmental Grantmakers Association. In all, billions of dollars fund these NGO campaigns.

Through this very system, Sustainable Development has grown from a collection of ideas and wish lists of an extensive variety of private organizations and global bureaucrats to become the most widely implemented tool in the UNs quest for global governance.

WHO ARE THE NGOS?

The three most powerful organizations influencing United Nations Environmental Program policy are three international NGOs. They are the World Wide Fund for Nature (WWF), the World Resources Institute (WRI) and the International Union for Conservation and Nature (IUCN). These three organizations provide the philosophy, objectives, and methodology for the international environmental agenda through a series of official reports and studies such as: *World Conservation Strategy*, published in 1980 by all three groups; *Global Biodiversity Strategy*, published in 1992; and *Global Biodiversity Assessment*, published in 1996.

These groups not only influence, UNEP's agenda, they also influence a staggering array of international and national NGOs around the world. Jay Hair, former head of the National Wildlife Federation, one of the U.S.'s largest environmental organizations, was also the president of the IUCN. Hair later turned up as co-chairman of President Clinton's Council on Sustainable Development.

The WWF maintains a network of national chapters around the world which influence if not dominate, NGO activities at the national level. It is at the national level where NGOs agitate and lobby national governments to implement the policies that the IUCN, WWF, and WRI get written into the documents that are advanced by the UNEP. In this manner, the world grows ever closer to global governance.

Other than treaties, how does UNEP policy become U.S. policy? Specifically, the IUCN membership includes an incredible mix of U.S. government agencies along with major U.S. NGOs. Federal agencies include the Department of State, Department of Interior, Department of Agriculture, Environmental Protection Agency (EPA), the National Park Service (NPS) the U.S. Forest Service (USFS), and the Fish and Wildlife Service. These agencies send representatives to all meetings of the UNEP.

Also attending those meetings as active members are NGO representatives. These include activist groups such as the Environmental Defense Fund, National Audubon Society, The Nature Conservancy, National

Wildlife Federation, Zero Population Growth, Planned Parenthood, the Sierra Club, the National Education Association, Greenpeace International, Green Cross International (started by former Soviet leader Gorbachev), the National Association for the Advancement of Colored People (NAACP) and hundreds more.

Other groups work in tandem with the official NGOs as ground troops in the cities. Some are planning groups, like the American Planning Association (APA), which operates not only in nearly every community in the nation, but in every university and college. Some are land trusts, usually operating on the local level, such as the Piedmont Environmental Council (PEC), which is a major player in at least nine counties in Virginia, with direct connections in several other states.

Every community has its own versions of the APA and PEC. These groups all have specific political agendas of which they pressure government officials into making local or state laws. Through their official contact with government agencies, working side-by-side with the UNEP, they eventually get their way.

One of the key NGO groups operating in major Americans cities is the International Council for Local Environmental Initiatives (ICLEI). Today, the group just calls itself ICLEI – Local Governments for Sustainability.

In 1992, ICLEI was one of the dominant groups helping to create Agenda 21. After the Earth Summit, ICLEI set bringing Agenda 21 policy into every city in the world as its goal. Within ten years more than 650 U.S. cities were paying dues from taxpayer funds to ICLEI so it could provide the needed tools to reorganize local government to incorporate Sustainable Development policies into nearly every local decision process.

ICLEI provided software programs to help set the goals for community development, brought in a team of "Green" experts, newsletters, case studies, fact sheets, practice manuals, conferences and workshops to train local government staffs to only think in terms of sustainable policy. ICLE would then recommend that the local government hire a "sustainability manager" to oversee it all. Through this process, ICLEI and other NGO groups have been able to dictate policy, while staying hidden in the backrooms of local government.

HOW THE NGO WISH LIST BECOMES LAW

How can this be, you ask? How can private organizations control policy and share power equal to elected officials? Here's how it works.

When the dust settled over the 1992 Rio Earth Summit, five major documents were forced into international policy that could change forever how national policy is made. The Rio Summit was official named the United Nations Conference on Environment and Development (UNCED). That Conference outlined a new procedure for shaping policy. The procedure is called "soft law" policy, meaning it is not a treaty that must be ratified by national governments. In this way proponents of the policy can say such plans, like Agenda 21, have no enforcement capability. They insist soft law policy is just a suggestion – to be voluntarily implemented by each nation. It is perhaps best described as "controlled consensus" or "affirmative acquiescence." However, the introduction as soft law consensus is only the first step in the process.

The UNCED procedure utilizes four elements of power: international government (UN), national governments, non-governmental organizations, and philanthropic institutions.

The NGOs are the key to creating policy. The UN first sponsors an NGO forum designed specifically to bring NGO activists into the process. There they are fully briefed on the policy and then trained to prepare papers representing their own organization's private agendas to include in the proposed policy ideas. In addition the NGOs are trained to lobby and influence the official delegates of an upcoming regional conference. The policy ideas are accepted at the regional level by one or more UN organizations to serve as policy sponsor as it moves up the ladder. That organization may then re-work the language of the raw proposal to be more vague and less-threatening in its purpose. Finally, the all-important international conference is held, often attended by heads of state. The NGO policy, with the new language, is then presented to the conference delegates. The NGOs use their training to influence the delegates to accept the documents. In this way, the NGOs have developed the policy, controlled the debate, and assured it is adopted.

The ultimate goal of the conference is to produce a "Convention," which is a legally-drawn policy statement on specific issues. Once the "Convention" is adopted by the delegates, it is sent to the national governments for official ratification. Major policy documents are usually saved for presentation at international conferences where, with great fanfare, they are signed by the attending heads of state of UN member nations. Once that is done, the new policy is on its way to becoming international law. At the 1992 Rio Earth Summit where Agenda 21 was introduced, President George H.W. Bush signed the document for the U.S. Because it was deemed a soft law policy it was not required to be ratified by Congress. In 2016, Barack Obama played a similar strategy in signing the Paris Climate Change Accord, thus avoiding the need for Congress to ratify it.

Once the documents are signed by the heads of state, the real work begins. Compliance to the signed agreement must be assured. Again, the NGOs come into the picture. They are responsible for pressuring Congress to write national laws and regulatory policy to comply with the treaty. One trick used to assure compliance is to write into the laws the concept of third-party lawsuits.

NGOs now regularly sue the government and private citizens to force policy. Their legal fees and even damage awards are paid to them out of the government treasury, but because the government nearly always settles before the case gets to court, there is no paper trail of what took place. Through a coordinated process, hundreds of NGOs are at work in Congress, in every state government, and in every local community advancing some component of the global environmental agenda.

However, the United States Constitution's Tenth Amendment bars the federal government from writing laws that dictate specific local policy. To bypass this roadblock, NGOs encourage Congress to include special grant programs that include strict compliance to the desired policy. The grants are then offered to the states and communities on a "voluntary" basis. Therefore it's not a specific rule or law that they comply with – it's just their choice, should they want to accept the grant. Yet, the desired policy is enforced through compliance with stipulations written into the grants.

If a community or state does refuse to participate "voluntarily," there's a special strategy ready and waiting for them. Local chapters of the NGOs are trained to go into action. They begin to pressure city councils or county commissioners to accept the grants and implement the policy. Should they meet resistance, one tactic is to issue news releases telling the residents of the community their elected officials are losing millions of their own tax dollars that should rightfully be spent improving the hometown. The pressure continues until it "convinces" the local officials to give in and take the grant.

That's how policies like Agenda 21's Sustainable Development goals go from a "suggestion" (as claimed by the UN and its NGO matrix) to control through the power of law. The truth is the debate over environmental issues has very little to do with clean water and air and much more to do with the establishment of power. NGOs are gaining power as locally elected officials are losing it. The result is that the structure of American government is being systematically changed to accommodate the private agendas of NGOs. In addition, many of the leaders of the NGO organizations are being given government positions in counties, cities, and towns that they have been instrumental in conspiring against. They label themselves "stakeholders."

Put in simple street language, the procedure really amounts to a collection of NGOs, bureaucrats, and government officials, all working together toward a predetermined outcome. They meet, write policy statements based on the international agreements which they helped to create, produce "voluntary" grant programs complete with specific language that make their plans mandatory, and so create laws and regulations that will enforce the "voluntary" suggestions into national, state, and local law.

This is their slick, silent, yet ultimately controlling procedure that insures the desired outcome without the ugliness of bloodshed -- or even debate. It is the procedure used to advance the radical, global environmental agenda of Sustainable Development.

CHAPTER NINE

SELLING THE INTERNATIONAL AGENDA AS "LOCAL"

As Agenda 21 was introduced to the world in 1992 to be the Comprehensive Blueprint for reorganizing human society, a few activists, your author included, began an effort to sound the alarm about this very dangerous plan. We were, of course, attacked, derided, ridiculed, and even ignored as we were systematically labeled as tinfoil hat-wearing, conspiracy theory nut cases.

We didn't stop, and over the years, as the policies began to take their toll, some Americans began to heed our warnings and take them to heart. Local residents started attending town council meetings, listening and asking questions. Were these elected officials actually enforcing international UN policies?

At first, the local officials were puzzled by the questions. International? No, of course not. These are all LOCAL!!! They were caught unaware of the origins of such policies because the NGOs and planners working with them in the backrooms had never mentioned anything called Agenda 21. So, no, of course not, came their answer.

Eventually, our resistance grew stronger. Now the NGOs could no longer ignore us. They were forced to fight back openly. First, they admitted something called Agenda 21 existed, but said it was simply a suggestion for organizing development while protecting the environment. "Agenda 21," they said, "has no enforcement capability." Their most often used "new" description of Agenda 21 was an "innocuous, 20 year old document that had no enforcement power." Nothing to worry about.

Then, as our resistance continued to grow, they turned to sarcasm, "There are no Blue Helmeted Troops at city hall!"

As the battle increased, the Sustainablists began to rely more and more on planners with no visible connection to the UN. The American Planning Association is the premier planning group operating in nearly every community. It is trusted by elected officials as a responsible force for sound city planning. The APA is counted on to provide good, solid, honest, workable ideas to help the cities plan for the future. And most important of all, they have no direct political ties with the United Nations or any conspiracy theories like the so-called Agenda 21! Here is a group you can trust.

As planning meetings across the nation came under siege from anti-Agenda 21 citizens, eventually the APA, too, had to respond to assure the public it was all a lie. There was "no hidden agenda" in their local plans!

First, on its website, the APA provided a section called "Agenda 21: Myths and Facts. There, the APA goes to extreme measures to distance itself and its policies from Agenda 21, specifically stating, "The American Planning Association has no affiliation regarding any policy goals and recommendations of the UN." That statement alone is interesting since the APA uses the term "sustainable," which has its incontrovertible origins from the UN.

Directly related to that point, it would be interesting to hear the APA explain some information found in one of its own documents from 1994. The document was an APA newsletter to its members in the Northern California (San Francisco) area. The article was a commentary entitled "How Sustainable is Our Planning," by Robert Odland. It was written just two years after the UN Earth Summit at which Agenda 21 was first introduced to the world. The fifth paragraph of the article states:

"Vice President Gore's book, Earth in the Balance addressed many of the general issues of sustainability. Within the past year, the President's Council on Sustainable Development has been organized to develop recommendations for incorporating sustainability into the federal government. Also, various groups have been formed to implement Agenda 21, a comprehensive blueprint for sustainable development that was adopted at the recent UNCED conference in Rio de Janeiro (the "Earth Summit").

In that one paragraph, this document brings together the APA, Agenda 21, the UN's Earth Summit, Al Gore, Sustainable Development, the President's Council on Sustainable Development, NGO groups with the mission of implementing Agenda 21 and the description of Agenda 21 as a "Comprehensive Blueprint" for Sustainable planning.

A couple of paragraphs higher in the article, it says, "*A common misconception is that sustainability is synonymous with self-sufficiency; on the contrary, sustainability must recognize the interconnections between different levels of societal structure.*" That "societal structure" is "social justice," as described in Agenda 21.

The American Planning Association is part of the Planners Network. The network is officially run by a group called the Organization of Progressive Planners. According to the Network's website, it's "an association of professionals, activists, academics, and students involved in physical, social, economic, and environmental planning in urban and rural areas, who promote fundamental change in our political and economic systems."

A visit to the website PlannersNetwork.org, one will find in its Statement of Principles this quote: "*We believe planning should be a tool for allocating resources…and eliminating the great inequalities of wealth and power in our society … because the free market has proven incapable of doing this.*"

That statement is advocating redistribution of wealth, social justice and social engineering. That, then, is what nearly every planning group in nearly every community advocate in their planning programs. It is clearly the official policy of the American Planning Association. Still the APA insists that its planning has nothing to do with Agenda 21.

As already shown, the United Nations blatantly advocates that Capitalism and private property rights are not sustainable, and thus pose the greatest threat to the world's ecosystem and social equity. And, while sometimes using different words, the APA is helping communities across the nation enforce these ideas, while swearing each is a local idea, designed from local input. So how is it possible that every town and county has come up with the exact same idea at the same time? The answer obviously is that they are all using the same planners concepts from the same planners – the APA.

As George Orwell masterfully put it in his epic novel "Animal Farm," it's become difficult to see the difference between the pigs and the farmers – or the APA and the UN.

Sustainable Development is not implemented in the open, as the APA claims, but in backrooms filled with the proper NGOs which surround your elected officials and pressures their actions. In that way Sustainable Development is changing our American society and form of government, making government more powerful and more invasive in our daily lives as it moves further from the control of the people.

TACTICS USED BY THE AMERICAN PLANNING ASSOCIATION

Okay, let's get down to the nitty-gritty. How do planning groups like the APA really control opinions and gain support for their planning ideas? How do they overcome the fears as they impose plans that destroy private property and change the entire structure of the community?

Here's a recent example:

With great fanfare, the American Planning Association (APA) reported results of a survey the group conducted, "Planning America: Perceptions and Priorities," showing that the anti-Agenda 21 "crowd is slim." Said the report, only 6% of those surveyed expressed opposition to Agenda 21, while 9% expressed support for Agenda 21 and 85%, "the vast majority of respondents, don't know about Agenda 21."

Typically, APA is using the survey to formulate the image that opponents to Agenda 21/Sustainable Development are just a lunatic fringe with no standing and of no consequence in the "real" world. They continue to portray Agenda 21 as simply a 20-year-old idea, and just a suggestion that planners and local governments might consider.

However, a closer look at the full survey, plus additional APA reports reveal some interesting, and, in some cases, astounding facts.

First the survey:

It was designed to show support for "Planning." This has become an obsession with the "planning community" because of the growing opposition to Agenda 21 and Sustainable Development.

According to the APA, the findings of the Survey reveal that: Only one-third believe their communities are doing enough to address economic situations; it says that very few Americans believe that market forces alone (the free market) improve the economy or encourage job growth; 84 % feel that their community is getting worse or staying the same; Community planning is seen as needed by a wide majority of all demographics; and of course, that 85% of Americans just don't know enough to hold an opinion about Agenda 21.

Those are pretty astounding findings. It looks like these "honest" planners have their fingers on the pulse of the nation. Surprising perhaps, until you look at the actual questions asked in the survey. For example, Finding #4: Community planning is seen as needed by a wide majority of all demographics (79% agree; 9% disagree; and 12% don't know). Wow!

But here is the actual question that was asked: "Generally, do you agree or disagree that your community could benefit from a community plan as defined above?" The definition provided in order to answer the question was this: "Community planning is a process that seeks to engage all members of a community to create more prosperous, convenient, equitable, healthy and attractive places for present and future generations."

Asking the question in that manner is akin to holding up a picture of Marilyn Monroe along side one of Rosie O'Donnell and asking which one would they want to date. Give me the pretty one please – say 79%. In fact, in some actual planning meetings they do just that – hold up a picture of the downtown area depicting decaying, dreary buildings versus one of a shining, beautiful utopia, and they literally say, "which one do you want?" If the answer is (of course) the pretty one, then, YES, the community supports planning! Talk about a "dumbed-down" process.

Of course, the American Planning Association adamantly denies any connection to the United Nation's policy of Agenda 21 and its planning programs. So, how strange is it then, that the APA definition of planning (as stated above) is almost identical to the definition used by the UN to define Sustainable Development?

Here is the UN's definition of Sustainable Development: "Development that meets the needs of today without compromising the ability of future generations to meet their own needs." The UN further defines Agenda 21: "Effective execution of Agenda 21 will require a profound reorientation of all human society, unlike anything the world has ever experienced."

Such a forced policy would certainly "engage all members of a community" whether they want to be or not. The UN calls it a "redeployment of human resources." Other than semantics, there is no difference in the APA's and the UN's definitions of planning." The planners' definition uses an interesting term, "equitable." The UN also uses such a term in describing Agenda 21 – "Social Equity." And that is translated into another term: "Social Justice." It means "redistribution of wealth." Is that what the "local" planners have in mind for your community development?

It's obvious that the APA is playing word games with its surveys and definitions of planning. No wonder such an overwhelming majority answer in the affirmative to such questions. And, yes, maybe a lot of Americans don't know what Agenda 21 really is. However, if the APA asked real questions that gave a solid clue as to the planning they actually have in mind, it's fairly certain they would get a much different response – whether the person answering had ever heard of Agenda 21 or not.

For example, listed below are some sample questions that could help the APA take the real pulse of the community – if they wanted to be honest.

6 REAL QUESTIONS PLANNERS SHOULD ASK THE PUBLIC

1.   How do the citizens feel about planning policy that dictates the size of their yard which forces high-density developments where one practically sits on top of their neighbors? Do they still support such "Planning?"

2.   How do the citizens feel about planning that enforces the creation of light rail public transportation with a limited number of riders – yet could cost taxpayers so much money that it would be literally cheaper to buy each potential rider a brand new Rolls Royce, and even throw in the chauffeur for good measure? Do they still support such "Planning?"

3.   How do the citizens feel about planning that enforces limits on energy use, driving up energy costs? What if that included forcing residents to replace their appliances with more energy–efficient ones to meet "Planning Standards?" Do they still support such "Planning?"

4.   How do the citizens feel about planning that forces cars to "share the road" with bicycles and foot traffic, even as Planners narrow the streets, deliberately making it harder to drive? Do they still support such "Planning?"

5.   How do the citizens feel about planning that forces taxpayers to pay for plug-in stations for electric cars that hardly anyone wants or uses, for the specific purpose of forcing people to buy electric cars? Do they still support such "Planning?"

6.   How do the citizens feel about planning that creates non-elected boards, councils, and regional governments to enforce their policies, which actually diminish the power of the local officials they elected, severely reducing citizen input into policy? Do they still support such "Planning?"

Challenge planners to ask the questions in this manner instead of trying to whitewash them into sounding like innocent, non-intrusive local ideas for community development. Ask the questions so that they reflect the consequences of the plans, and then see if the 85% now are so eager to ignore the effects of Agenda 21.

The reality is that Americans across the nation are now openly protesting such policies that are being enforced in communities everywhere. They are directly tied to the stated goals of Sustainable Development, the official policy of Agenda 21. And that is why a twenty-five-year old "suggestion" has become the focal point of attacks on "local" planning.

Planners are shocked that people are opposed to such enforcement of policies that damage their private property and their pocketbooks, and they are doing everything possible to label such Americans as "fringe conspiracy theorists." The intentional bias of the survey is part of that effort.

As mentioned, the APA has organized a bootcamp to train their planners how to combat those nasty protestors. Through its new training, the APA downplays revealing details of the plan. Instead, they train planners to suggest ways to make their presentations merely "conversations with the community," using empathy and terms that are non-technical."

Obviously APA believes the protestors are just simple-minded and unable to see their wisdom. One shouldn't be so upset over losing control of their property, their business, or their farm. There's a higher good at stake here, after all.

And so, to accomplish that task of dumbed-down "planning," (and in fact, hiding its real purpose) the APA has gone to great lengths to change the words. For example, the APA has issued to its members a "Glossary for the Public" that suggests what words should no longer be used in public meetings when discussing planning. Don't use these words, they warn planners, because they make the opposition see "red." So the planners should not use words like collaboration and consensus, or public visioning, or even "Smart Growth."

The Glossary provides specific language and tactics to be used to defuse protests. "Stay on message," it says. "The following phrases may be useful to help you frame your message in a way that is positive and inclusive, when transitioning to a local example, or to stay on message during public meetings where critics may attempt to distract from the agenda or topic at hand." And here is the language they suggest: "Plans and planning are time-tested ways for communities and neighborhoods to create more options and choices for their residents…" In other words, we've always had planning, so what's the problem?"

Such "public" meetings that the APA is so worried about being disrupted are not public at all. They are usually "consensus" meetings, run by professional facilitators, trained in psychology to use stealth in order to direct the audience into a pre-determined direction for a pre-determined outcome. Anyone asking questions outside the well-controlled box is labeled a protestor. Do you support such artful tactics which are intended to silence opposition? Is this how public policy is made in a free society? What if that policy affects your property? Do you still want to say it's okay?

Yes, there have been attempts at minor planning in some communities throughout the history of America. One of the first was in Chicago in 1909, the first metropolitan city in the country. Many communities have worked to come up with efficient ways to deal with water use and waste disposal, and to assure that factories weren't built next door to private homes, and so forth. And no one is protesting that! Private property protection was almost always a central concern. In states like Montana, there was no planning, and it has worked well for them.

This fight is with "planning" that is specifically designed to curtail energy use, drive up costs, control private property and development and building -- literally dictating changes in our lives and even changing the very structure of our system of government.

One of the planning tools the APA uses to enforce Sustainability is the International Code Council (ICC), an international set of standards based on a one size fits all set of regulations. The ICC also develops the International Energy Conservation Code, a model for energy efficiency codes used in planning. And it develops a standard for Accessible and Usable Building Facilities. In addition, most communities are now adding enforcement of International Building Codes (IBC) to development plans. Each of these codes is aimed at cutting back energy use, controlling private property use, and -- in short -- enforcing Sustainable Development.

Remember where the concept of Sustainable Development was first introduced and perfected as an agenda for development? Oh yes, in Agenda 21. As international codes are enforced on local communities using the consensus process, there is no room for discussion, reason, or consideration for exceptional local situations. The APA brings these codes and others into the community planning as a pre-packaged deal inflicting the community with (yes) foreign regulations. And, yes, dedicated Americans are protesting that this is not local government or planning, but the enforcement of an international (UN) agenda.

And so it goes. Government in the U.S., at all levels, is rapidly moving forward with such plans in every community, using the NGO ground troops and the plans supplied by the American Planning Association, and fueled by compliance to the rules in the federal grants. It's happening fast, and is all-pervasive. And as people are being run over by such plans, some are trying to slow down the runaway freight train by standing in the tracks and yelling stop! They of course are the ones labeled as fringe nuts.

However, as the APA does everything it can to so label such opponents to their plans, a shocking new report provides evidence that the sustainable polices advocated by APA in the cities – the policy known as Smart Growth – is wrong-headed and really pretty dumb. And where does such a report appear? Here's the real shocker. It was published in the Journal of the American Planning Association in an article entitled "Does Urban Form Really Matter." It is an analysis of Smart Growth polices showing that the "compact city" controls don't work.

Says the report in its final summation paragraph: "*The current planning policy strategies for land use and transportation have* **virtually no impact** *on the major long-term increases in resource and energy consumption. They will generally tend to* **increase costs** *and* **reduce economic competitiveness**... *In many cases, the socioeconomic* **consequences of less housing choices**, *crowding, and congestion may* **outweigh** *the very* **modest** *CO2 reduction benefits.*"

There you have it. Right out of the pages of the APA's own Journal, the very policies that they are forcing on communities across the nation, are wrong. They don't work! Forcing mass migration into cities, where people are to live in high-density buildings or homes on lots so close together that the dog can't squeeze between houses, has no effect on the environment. The fact is, Sustainable "planning" creates an artificial shortage of land, causing housing costs to go up. It doesn't cut down on energy use or protect the environment. It's a dishonest and useless intrusion in the lives of all Americans.

And that is exactly why protests are building against Agenda 21. Because it is wrong. The premise is wrong. The facts, as presented by the APA and other planners, are wrong. It is wrong for our nation. Wrong for property owners. Wrong for future generations.

In the 1970s, author Richard Bach, who wrote the classic book, *Jonathan Livingston Seagull*, also wrote a second book entitled, *Illusions: The Adventures of a Reluctant Messiah*. In the book, a Messiah, forced to come up with answers to the problems of life, consulted the "Messiah's Handbook." All he had to do was open the book and it would miraculously turn to the very page containing the answer he sought. He stumbled through his adventures, following the handbook. But finally, in the end, as he consulted it one last time, the page read simply, "Everything in this book may be wrong."

There is only one right approach for a community to come together to discuss and solve common problems: open discussion, honest debates and votes, and above all, a full concentration on the protection of private property rights as the ultimate decider. The American Planning Association needs a new handbook!

CHAPTER TEN

THE KELO DECISION ORGANIZED THEFT

A nation based on the very concept of private property rights stands in the way of the Sustainable juggernaut. If property rights are upheld and protected, then there is no way for the scheme to succeed in the United States. However, this is a powerful global plan for reorganization of human civilization at stake here. The train is ready to leave the station, but the way is blocked by those infernal property rights! What to do?

There has to be a way to harmonize the United States into accepting the goal. Just be patient and clever. The answer? Five black robes named Stevens, Souter, Ginsburg, Kennedy, and Breyer.

In 2005, the Supreme Court of the United States handed down an opinion that shocked the nation. It was the case of *Susette Kelo, et al. v City of New London, Connecticut, et al.* The issue: "The government taking of property from one private owner to give to another private entity for economic development constitutes a permissible "public use" under the Fifth Amendment."

In 2000, the city of New London saw a chance to rake in big bucks through tax revenues for a new downtown development project that was to be anchored by pharmaceutical giant Pfizer. The company announced a plan to build a $270 million dollar global research facility in the city. The local government jumped at the chance to transform 90 acres of an area right next to the proposed research facility. Their plans called for the creation of the Fort Trumbull development project to provide hotels, housing and shopping areas for the expected influx of Pfizer employees. There were going to be jobs and revenues A-Go-Go in New London. Just one obstacle stood in the way of these grand plans. There were private homes in that space.

No muss – no fuss. The city fathers had a valuable tool in their favor. They would just issue an edict that they were taking the land by eminent domain. The city created a private development corporation to lead the project. First priority for the new corporation was to obtain the needed property.

Put yourself in the shoes of the homeowners in that quaint neighborhood, with its view of the bay. You bought a home for your family. It might even have been handed down by your father or grandfather. It's a place you could afford in a neighborhood you like. The children made friends. You intended to stay for the rest of your life.

However, as you planted your garden, landscaped the yard, put up a swing set for the kids, and molded your land into a home, unknown to you, certain city officials were meeting around a table with developers. In front of them were maps, plats and photographs of your home. They talked of dollars. Big dollars. Tax revenues for the city, huge profits for the developer. Expensive condos, hotels, and a shopping center with all the trimmings began to take shape. You weren't asked for input or permission. You weren't even notified that your home was targeted until the whole project was finalized and the only minor detail was to get rid of you. But they can't just take your house because it belongs to you. There are laws to protect you. And you weren't planning to go anywhere. Let em try!

Susette Kelo bought a nice little pink house in a quiet neighborhood in New London. Little did she imagine that warm, comfy place would soon become the center of a firestorm.

She had no intention of selling. She'd spent a considerable amount of money and time fixing up her little pink house, a home with a beautiful view of the water that she could afford. She planted flowers in the yard, braided her own rugs for the floors, filled the rooms with antiques and created the home she wanted.

Less than a year later, the trouble started. A real estate broker suddenly showed up on her door representing an unknown client. Suzette said she wasn't interested in selling. The realtor's demeanor then changed as she warned that the property was going to be condemned by the city. Then, one year later, on the day before Thanksgiving, the sheriff taped a letter to her door, stating that her home had been condemned by the City of New London.

Then the pressure began. A notice came in the mail telling her that the city intended to take her land. An offer of compensation was made, but it was below the market price. The explanation given was that, since the government was going to take the land, it was no longer worth the old market price. Therefore the lower price was "just compensation," as called for in the Fifth Amendment. It was a "fair price," the homeowners were told over and over.

Some neighbors quickly gave up, took the money and moved away. With the loss of each one, the pressure mounted. Visits from government agents became routine. They knocked on the door at all hours, demanding her sell. Newspaper articles depicted her as unreasonably holding up community progress. They called her greedy. Finally, the bulldozers moved in on the properties already sold. As they crushed down the houses, the neighborhood became unlivable. It looked like a war zone.

In Susette Kelo's neighborhood, the imposing bulldozer was sadistically parked in front of a house, waiting. The homeowner came under great pressure to sell. More phone calls, threatening letters, visits by city officials at all hours, demanding they sign the contract to sell. It just didn't stop. Finally the intimidation began to break down the most dedicated homeowner's resolve. In tears, they gave in and sold. Amazingly, once they sold, the homeowners were then classified as "willing sellers!"

Immediately that house was bulldozed and then the monster machine was moved next door to the next house, sitting there like a huffing, puffing dragon, ready to strike.

Finally Susette's little pink house stood nearly alone in the middle of a destruction site. Over 80 homes were gone, seven remained. As if under attack by a conquering army, she was finally surrounded, with no place to run but to the courts. The United States was built on the very premise of the protection of private property rights. How could a government possibly be allowed to take anyone's home for private gain? Surely justice would finally prevail.

Under any circumstances the actions of the New London government and its sham development corporation should have been considered criminal behavior. It used to be. If city officials were caught padding their own pockets, or those of their friends, it was considered graft. That's why RICO laws were created.

Finally, her case was heard by the highest court in the land. It was such an obvious case of government overreach against private property owners that no one considered there was a chance of New London winning. The city was backed in its appeal by the National League of Cities, one of the largest proponents of eminent domain use, saying the policy was critical to spurring urban renewal with development projects.

Property Rights legal foundations, in particular, the Institute for Justice, came to Susette's rescue to serve as her advocate before the high court. They were joined by a wide array of groups such as the American Association of Retired People (AARP), and the late Martin Luther Kings' Southern Christian Leadership Conference. Truly this was seen as a civil rights case.

The National Association for the Advancement of Colored People (NAACP) filed an amicus brief arguing that eminent domain has often been used against politically weak communities with high concentrations of minorities and elderly.

The Supreme Court had always stood with the founders of the nation on the vital importance of private property. There was precedent after precedent to back up the optimism that they would do so again. However, to the shock of everyone involved, private property rights sustained a near death blow that day.

This time, five black robes named Stevens, Souter, Ginsburg, Kennedy, and Breyer shocked the nation by ruling that officials who had behaved like Tony Soprano were in the right and Susette Kelo had no ground to stand on, literally or figuratively.

These four men and one woman ruled that the United States Constitution is meaningless as a tool to protect individuals against the wants and desires of government. Their ruling in the Kelo case declared that Americans own nothing. After deciding that any property is subject to the whim of a government official, it was just a short trip to declaring that government could now confiscate anything we own, anything we create, anything we've worked for – in the name of an undefined common good.

In defending the decision, Justice Stevens simply wrote, "Promoting economic development is a traditional and long accepted function of government." He mentioned not a word about the long tradition of government in the United States that had always stood for the rights of the individual. Not surprisingly, *The New York Times* and *The Washington Post* supported the decision.

Justice Sandra Day O'Conner, who opposed the Court's decision, vigorously rebutted Stevens' argument, as she wrote in dissent of the majority opinion, "The specter of condemnation hangs over all property. Nothing is to prevent the state from replacing a Motel 6 with a Ritz-Carlton, any home with a shopping mall, or any farm with a factory."

Justice Clarence Thomas issued his own rebuttal to the decision, specifically attacking the argument that this was a case about "public use." He accused the Majority of replacing the Fifth Amendment's "Public Use" clause with a very different "Public Purpose" test. Said Justice Thomas "This deferential shift in phraseology enables the Court to hold against all common sense, that a costly urban-renewal project whose stated purpose is a vague promise of new jobs and increased tax revenue, but which is also suspiciously agreeable to the Pfizer Corporation, is for a **public use.**"

Incredibly, after the Supreme Court decision that literally destroyed the nation's oldest and most revered right of private property ownership, it turned out that the entire action by the New London government had been for absolutely nothing. There was no great "revitalization" of downtown. No jobs. No development. Nope. The New London development was never completed. The proposed hotel-retail-condo "urban village" was never built. The developer failed to come up with the necessary funds. Pfizer, whose employees were supposed to be the clientele for the project, pulled out and abandoned their planned research facility. Instead they decided to merge with a new partner, Wyeth. Rather than completing the New London project, the two pharmaceutical giants decided to create a combined facility in another city. They took the 1,500 jobs with them.

The land where Susette Kelo's little pink house once stood remains undeveloped to this day. In the aftermath of 2011's Hurricane Irene, the now-closed New London redevelopment area was turned into a dump for storm debris such as tree branches and other vegetation. No tax revenues are generated by the now-wasteland of government greed. But the precedent of the Kelo decision for government takings of land across the nation has grown to unimaginable levels.

Astonishingly the members of the Supreme Court have no other job but to protect the Constitution and defend it from bad legislation. They sit in their lofty ivory tower, with their life-time appointments, never actually having to worry about job security or the need to answer to political pressure. Yet, these five black robes obviously missed finding a single copy of the Federalist Papers, which were written by many of the Founders to explain to the American people how they envisioned the new government was to work. In addition, they apparently missed the collected writings of James Madison, Thomas Jefferson, John Adams and George Washington, just to mention a very few. It's obvious because otherwise, there is simply no way they could have reached this decision.

So how did Stevens, Souter, Ginsburg, Kennedy, and Breyer miss such a rock solid foundation of American law? Perhaps they didn't. Perhaps they chose to ignore it in favor of another agenda. Specifically, Agenda 21, and the growing enforcement of Sustainable Development.

For several years, certain members of the Supreme Court have been discussing the need to review international law and foreign court decisions to determine U.S. Supreme Court rulings. Justice Breyer has been the most outspoken for this policy, saying, "We face an increasing number of domestic legal questions that directly implicate foreign or international law."

What international laws are these? In general, the most pervasive are a series of UN international treaties, including several that address issues of climate change, resource use, biological diversity, and community development. However, it was the policy of Sustainable Development, as expressed in Agenda 21, which served as their guide, as the document expresses specific goals and a tight timetable for implementation.

To fully understand the urgency for the Kelo decision, it's important to note that, at the same time the Supreme Court was hearing the Kelo case, in June, 2005, the UN held a major gathering in San Francisco where the mayors of cities from across the nation and around the world gathered to pledge that they would impose Sustainable polices. As the Supreme Court prepared its opinion, there was great activity underway across the nation to meet the goals set by federal, state and local governments to impose the guidelines set in place by the President's Council on Sustainable Development. There were regulatory demands with which to comply. There was grant money dangling in front of greedy officials. There was a brave new world to unfold in the land of the ever-growing power of government.

The use of Eminent Domain was becoming the favored tool. Sustainable Development created the governmentally unhealthy, but prosperous partnerships between the public sector (your local government) and private businesses, just as was done in Now London. But the symbol of Susette Kelo's infernal pink house could upset the entire apple cart if she were to win the court case and force governments to protect private property rights.

In fact, loud voices of protest against the brutal, organized theft via Sustainable practices were beginning to rise across the nation. Many Americans had started to fight back to protect their property.

» In Oregon, people went to the ballot box and shocked lawmakers by passing Measure 37, which said the government must either pay full price for any land taken or waive the regulation and leave the property owner alone.

» In Wisconsin, the state legislature passed a bill to stop Smart Growth policies that were destroying property owners.

» In Michigan, the state Supreme Court overturned the precedent-setting ruling it had made more than 20 years earlier that allowed the use of eminent domain in taking property for private use. In fact, it was that original ruling that had been used by communities across the nation to justify their own eminent domain takings.

Clearly, many states in the nation had started to rise up to stop this assault on private property. Without the power to grab property at will, the ability for government to enforce Sustainable Development was under threat. Again, it was those pesky Founders and their old fashioned ideas about property rights. No other nation needed to put up with these kinds of controls. Other governments just took it!

Those who supported Sustainable Development and Agenda 21 needed something big to put things back on track. The Supreme Court, which had already stated that it must look to international laws and treaties to decide American law, provided the answer. Can it be any clearer that, in making the Kelo decision, Stevens, Souter, Ginsburg, Kennedy, and Breyer chose Sustainable Development and Agenda 21 over the Constitution of the United States?

So, in a five to four vote, the Supreme Court said that it was okay for a community to use eminent domain to take land, shut down a business, or destroy and reorganize an entire neighborhood, *if* it benefited the community in a positive way. Specifically, "positive" meant unquestioned government control and more tax dollars.

Now, as the public/private partnerships between government and private developers move to enforce Sustainable Development in local communities, an unholy alliance is also forming. The "greasing of the palm" is an age-old tradition in order to get anything done in Third World countries. With the Kelo decision and its inevitable creation of public/private partnerships that combine power and money, the practice of palm-greasing has come to America. Corrupt politicians are lining their pockets as they gain political power by forming their own partnerships with select businesses and developers to build personal wealth and power. They plot to take land that isn't theirs for personal gain, while claiming it's for the "public good." Kelo, gave them all the power they needed to hide their true intent.

Property rights had to be pushed out of the way in order for Sustainable Development to move forward, changing our communities, our culture and our system of government. As opposition began to build, the five black robes stepped into the breach to slam the door on American property rights.

BUT THE BATTLE WASN'T OVER

Kelo was the shock heard around the country. Stunned officials in the federal government and elected officials in state and local entities weren't sure what the consequences would be. Americans who had rarely uttered a political thought were suddenly talking about property rights and government overreach. News programs and talk shows were focusing on the Fifth Amendment of the Constitution. It had been a long time since Americans had been so focused on their rights.

Was the Kelo case actually backfiring on the Sustainable agenda? Would it be overturned? As the decision's full meaning began to sink in state legislators took action by introducing legislation to change their eminent domain laws to help prevent another such property takings case.

Prior to the Kelo case only eight states specifically prohibited the use of eminent domain for economic development. These were Arkansas, Florida, Kansas, Kentucky, Maine, New Hampshire, South Carolina, and Washington. In the wake of Kelo, 42 states enacted some type of reform legislation. Twenty-two enacted laws that severely inhibit the takings allowed by the Kelo decision, while the rest enacted laws that provide some kind of limitation on the powers of communities to use eminent domain for economic development purposes.

Then Congress got into the act to protect property by limiting the use of eminent domain, introducing the Private Property Protection Act. The bill was introduced in the Senate by Senator John Cornyn, (R-TX) on June 27, 2005. The two most important features of the bill were:

» Prohibits the federal government from exercising eminent domain power if the only justifying "public use" is economic development; and
» Imposes the same limit on state and local government exercise of eminent domain power "through the use of Federal funds."

Finally here was the bill to completely reverse the damage of the Kelo decision. It is the proper reaction by Congress when an opinion handed down by the Supreme Court reveals bad or inappropriate government policy. Congress was moving to represent the people and uphold the Constitution. That's a rare moment, it seems, in modern history.

A version of the Property Rights Protection Act quickly passed the House of Representatives. All that remained was passage in the Senate. Was Agenda 21/Sustainable Development about to be stopped in the United States?

Clearly the Property Rights Protection Act was a direct threat to certain interest groups, specifically the National Conference of Mayors and the National League of Cities. Both groups represented the ground troops of Sustainable Development policy at the local level. The Kelo decision was to be a major weapon in their arsenal to build power and transform local government.

Smart Growth is the official policy of the U.S. Conference of Mayors, as is prominently displayed on the group's website. Alarmed that the Property Rights Protection Act might actually acknowledge that people have rights to their property, the U.S. Conference of Mayors issued an emergency resolution at its 74th Winter Meeting that underscored the use of eminent domain as integral to the economic development of local communities. Said the resolution, "Without the use of eminent domain it will be very difficult and/or expensive for many cities to carry out public/ private economic development." They meant, of course, difficult without a powerful sledgehammer over property owners.

The Mayors and the National League of Cities were terrified that their days of abusing property rights were coming to an end. To fight the new Congressional and state legislation which threatened their control over property, these two joined forces to delay any such attempts to legally stop them. It was the age-old tactic to let the storm pass, let it all calm down, let people forget. Then sneak their desired goals past the unsuspecting public. The Mayor's Resolution called on the federal government to take no further action to alter the rules governing eminent domain until it had; 1) received the report on the results of a study currently being conducted by the Government Accountability Office on how state and local governments are using eminent domain across the nation; 2) and held that Congress could hold comprehensive hearings. Delay.

Unfortunate for property owners, the battle for the right to own and control their land had fallen on the shrugging shoulders of Senator Arlen Specter (R-PA). The Senator was Chairman of the powerful Senate

Judiciary Committee, which would decide the fate of the Property Rights Protection Act, (S.1313). Specter was a big government boy all the way. You know, one of those guys who just naturally have the answers for how the rest of us should live. Senator Specter never saw a big government deal he didn't like. People, in Senator Specter's way of thinking, are just sheep to be coddled at election time. In Senator Specter's world, frivolous people who whine about losing their homes or jobs to government dictates just get in the way of serious work.

For the National Conference of Mayors and the National League of Cities, Senator Arlen Specter was the answer to their pleas. He simply had to do nothing. He just sat on the bill. No action was taken on the Property Rights Protection Act. Of course, the Senator didn't put it exactly in those terms. He assured us that he was just being cautious, reviewing the legislation. He didn't want to rush to judgment on so vital an issue.

He even held a hearing on the bill. It was, in fact, a very high profile one at that. He even allowed Suzette Kelo to take center stage and tell her story to the nation. The hearing was a brilliant delaying tactic. It made it look like Specter was actually doing something. But that was where all action stopped. All he had to do was wait. Once that session of Congress ended the bill would simply die.

What Senator Specter was perpetrating is a well-know legislative flimflam. While the nation is inflamed over the Court's decision, he just stalled, waiting for the furor to go away. Then he and his big government brethren could go back to business as usual.

So the Property Rights Protection Act died. In many of the states, the National Conference of Mayors and other group went to work to roll back or water down the property rights legislation that had been passed in the states. And Sustainable Development rolled on. Eminent domain remained the most valuable tool for the destruction of private property rights.

The Institute for Justice, the group that defended Suzette Kelo before the Supreme Court, reported that it found 10,000 cases in which condemnation was used or threatened for the benefit of private developers. These cases were all within a five-year period after the Kelo decision. Today, that figure is dwarfed as there is seemingly no limit on government takings of private property.

In 2017, the Supreme Court, again at the hands of Justice Kennedy, handed down another devastating blow to property owners in the case of *Joseph P. Murr et al v. State of Wisconsin and St. Croix County*. The Murr family owned two riverfront lots since the 1960s. One of the lots included a vacation home, the other was undeveloped.

The family wanted to sell the vacant lot to raise some money to upgrade the vacation house. The country told them no, selling the lots separately would violate a zoning law enacted to protect water quality. The family asked the county government to compensate them for the property's lost value, the county offered only $40,000, one tenth of the $400,000 assessed value. Murr argued that was a violation of the Fifth Amendment which requires "just compensation" when government takes private property for public use.

The case went to the U.S. Supreme court where the family lost the case in a 5-3 decision. In June, 2017, Justice Kennedy wrote for the majority "The government action was reasonable land-use regulation, enacted as part of a coordinated federal, state, and local effort to preserve the river and surrounding land... Courts must... define the parcel in a manner that reflects reasonable expectations about the property." In other words, land is no longer under the control of the owner who has a reasonable expectation of using it for his benefit. If government can come up with its own "reasonable" excuse, then it can just take it.

The Kelo decision changed the rules. The precedent was set. Land can now be taken anytime at the whim of a power elite. Mission accomplished.

CHAPTER ELEVEN

TOOLS FOR THE TRANSFORMATION
IN THE RURAL AREAS

So what are the most popular tools used by the land-grabbers in the name of promoting the drive for Sustainable control? It's a two-pronged attack: One for the cities and one for the rural areas. Hang on to your hats. The list is nearly endless, the corruption employed is breathtaking, and it's all taking place in your community, county and state.

The United States is a large land mass. While it contains major metropolitan areas like New York City, Chicago, and Los Angeles, it also features vast open areas, specifically in the west, including the Great Plains, the Rocky Mountains and deserts like the Sonora which covers over 100,000 square miles of territory.

Life in the megacities, compared to that in the rural areas, is a vastly different experience. Obviously the cities represent a more controlled version of society where food, housing and other essentials of life are stacked and packed into a limited area of access. One goes to the store, usually just down the street, buys the wanted items, and takes them home. Many residents of cities rarely even think about from whence such goods come. After working during the day at the job, residents have more time for leisure, perhaps to enjoy a play or a movie. Civilized, educated, cultured, are the terms most often used to describe many city dwellers.

Of course, the cities are also the location of a segment of society that is nearly cut off from the cultural aspect. These are the poor, perhaps strongly ethnic, neighborhoods where residents are nearly completely dependent on government for their existence, including income, housing, and food.

However, in the more rural areas of the nation, daily living can be a much different experience. Usually the convenience of necessary essentials is not down the street. Sometimes folks have to create their own. They grow crops on their farms, hunt, and cultivate livestock. These are the folks who create and provide much of the food for the cities, supply the building materials for the housing through timber, mining, and ranching. These are the so-called rugged individuals the image the American citizen was largely modeled after.

If the goal of the forces of Sustainable Development is to reorganize human society then, to succeed, there must be three very different plans, one for rural America and two for the cities to accomplish the job. Control of such vastly different cultural situations cannot be a one-size-fits all proposition.

Of course, it would be far simpler for the forces of control if everyone just lived the same way. Then only one plan would be necessary. Now, with the current cultural differences, how could such an idea be accomplished? Those rural people are so independent. Many live in the middle of nowhere. There's no way to know where they are or what they are doing at any given time. If only there were a way to just "herd" those rural people into the cities, then one force of power would be enough to control every aspect of life, from food to housing to keeping track of their every move.

Then the solution for full control came like a lightning flash! Control the land, the water, the air. Enforce strict regulations that literally make it impossible to live on the rural lands. Shut down rural livelihoods by targeting ranching, mining and the timber industry as threats to the environment. The rural residents would then have nowhere to go but to the cities. Perfect!

It was a dangerous plan that could backfire easily, especially when it affected such strong, independent-minded people who live on those plains and in the mountains. Of course they couldn't be so openly aggressive as to outright ban people from the land. Again, the mantra of Environmental Armageddon was the most useful tool. The Sustainablists, after all, were just trying to protect us all from ourselves.

So, one step at a time, and one program at a time, the agenda was put into place. In 1972, a grant from the Rockefeller Brothers Fund created the "preservationist agenda." William Reilly, who would later become Administrator of the EPA under George H.W. Bush, edited a document called The Use of Land: A Citizen's Policy Guide to Urban Growth. It called for changing the traditional view of land and how it was to be used. No longer would it be viewed as a commodity to be used for personal creation of wealth and individual empowerment. Rather, now land was to be considered sacred and using it for human purposes would only be considered when absolutely necessary – and only if tightly controlled.

The second document was prepared in 1977, entitled The Unfinished Agenda. Its purpose was to bring together sixty-three major environmental organizations to create a full agenda for controlling the land. These groups included the Sierra Club, Nature Conservancy, National Wildlife Federation, National Audubon Society, Population Growth, Friends of the Earth, and the Environmental Defense Fund.

These and many more, including international NGOs, would unite to use their power and money to influence government policy, create and oversee entire programs and file lawsuits to enforce it all. The modern, radical, activists Environmental Movement was born and their plan of action was set.

CHAPTER TWELVE

THE WILDLANDS PROJECT

"Our vision is simple, we live for the day when Grizzlies in Chihuahua have an unbroken connection to Grizzlies in Alaska; when gray wolf populations are continuous from New Mexico to Greenland." - Dave Foreman, leader of Earth First! and creator of the Wildlands Project

Earth First! emerged in the 1980s as one of the most radical of the environmental groups to begin carrying out the plan. They saw themselves as "Eco-Warriors," the *esprit de corp* of the radical environmental movement. To put an exclamation on their determination and boldness in their attitude, Earth First always included an ! at the end of their name. Earth First! had arrived to save the planet.

"Monkeywrenching was their tactic of choice. Sabotage! Earth First-er!s would go into the field of battle against the bulldozers and other tools of the timber and mining industries. Sugar in the gas tanks would render the hated machines useless. In addition, blowing up power transmission lines was another favorite tactic. Later they discovered a new, more effective means to stop the cutting of trees simply by rendering them useless to the timber industry. This was accomplished by driving large spikes into the trees. When the timber workers cut them down and shipped the trees to the sawmill for processing, the undetected spike would shred the saw. Production stopped. Cutting stopped. Victory for the Eco Warriors!

Of course, it's rarely mentioned in polite environmentalist circles about the time a millworker's face was destroyed when the saw he was operating hit a spike and exploded. War is hell, don't you know!

The chief spokesman and energetic co-founder of Earth First! was Dave Foreman. In 1985 he published the first edition of the book *Ecodefence: A Field Guide to Monkeywrenching*. It was a great help in recruiting more Eco Warriors to the cause and to teach them how to effectively sabotage private property.

Then Foreman came up with the mother of all plans. How were they to get control of that bothersome private property in the middle of all so much wilderness territory? Foreman created the Wildlands Project, a scheme to establish a network of protected wilderness areas across North America. He invented the term "rewilding," to define his plan to return the land back to the way it was before Christopher Columbus started the rush of settlement in North America. That, of course, would mean no human activity across vast amounts of the continent (of course, don't ask what the natives were doing there).

When Foreman first described his vision of a "rewilded" America in his book *Confessions of an Eco Warrior* only a few grasped the radical implications of his dream. The Wildlands Project is a massive program for restructuring society around nature. Nature was to be off-limits to man. No digging in the dirt to plant crops, no fences, no recreational vehicles, and no hunting. He best described it this way: "It is not enough to preserve the roadless, undeveloped country remaining. We must re-create wilderness in large regions: move out the cars and civilized people, dismantle the roads and dams, reclaim the plowed lands and clearcuts, -- reintroduce extirpated species." In reality, the Wildlands Project is a diabolical plan to herd people off the rural lands and into human settlements where they can be more effectively controlled.

In 1990, Foreman left Earth First! to formally establish the Wildlands Project. The concept was Foreman's, but the plan was developed by Dr. Reed Noss under grants from The Nature Conservancy and the National Audubon Society. That's when the project really took off.

As he took the lead in implementing the plan, Noss gave a grand description of what was to come, "The native ecosystems and the collective needs of non-human species must take precedence over the needs and desires of humans." There you have it. The plan to turn nature against man and man against himself as the radical environmental movement declared war against human society. That concept, in itself, was to become the most powerful tool ever conceived by the power mongers of history to take control of the world.

Under the Wildlands Project, "One half of the land area of the 48 conterminous (united) states be encompassed in core (wilderness) reserves and inner corridor zones (essentially extensions of core reserves) within the next few decades…Half of a region of wilderness is a reasonable guess of what it will take to restore viable populations of large carnivores and natural disturbance regimes, assuming that most of the other 50 percent is managed intelligently as buffer zones." Reed Noss,1992.

In published articles Foreman and Noss revealed the massive dimensions of their plan. They began by dividing the nation into what they called Core reserves. Core reserves are wilderness areas that supposedly allow biodiversity to flourish. "It is estimated," claimed Noss, "that large carnivores and ungulates require reserves on the scale of 2.5 to 25 million acres…for a minimum viable population of 1000 (large mammals), the figures would be 242 million acres for grizzly bears, 200 million acres for wolverines, and 100 million acres for wolves. Core reserves should be managed as roadless areas (wilderness). All roads should be permanently closed." Corridors are "extensions of reserves… Multiple corridors interconnecting a network of Core reserves provide functional redundancy and mitigate against disturbance… Corridors several miles wide are needed if the objective is to maintain resident populations of large carnivores."

Of course, there was no concern for the fact that those millions of acres included private property, ranches, industries, and whole communities. The ranches – those industries, those communities targeted for elimination, were the source of food and resources for the entire nation. It simply didn't matter to Forman, Noss, and their radical movement. Under the excuse of saving nature, such human activity was targeted for elimination.

While these ideas were dismissed by most as just the ravings of a few radicals, not to be taken seriously, again, let me remind you that the project was being funded by the very prim and proper Nature Conservancy and Audubon Society – the very public groups most people believed to be mainstream and responsible environmentalists. In fact, these groups were now joining hands with the most radical elements of their movement to actually take the land and destroy the human activity, completely contrary to the sovereign territory and the laws of the United States. The Wildlands Project would never have been taken seriously without the strong support of the mainstream environmental leadership.

In such a way, the movement was able to disguise its most radical elements and maintain an image of respectability, allowing most observers to completely underestimate the determination, indeed the power, of the movement that was forming under the banner of environmental protection.

A grant by the Ira Hiti Foundation for Deep Ecology provided the funds to publish and distribute 75,000 copies of the plan. The Wildlands Project was then set up as a corporation with offices in Arizona and Oregon; Foreman was Chairman of the Board and Reed Noss was made a Director. Armed with the funds and support of the movement's big boys, Foreman and Noss fanned out to spread their gospel of environmental control.

Next, Foreman and Noss teamed up their Wildlands Project with the Biosphere Reserve Program, a creation of the United Nations Educational, Scientific, and Cultural Organization (UNESCO). The objective of the Biosphere Reserve Program, conceived in 1971, had been to designate sites worldwide for preservation and to protect the biodiversity of chosen sites on a global level. So, in one quick move, the Wildlands Project quickly gained an official international footing.

Joining the effort, the Sierra Club created its own version of the map of North America, dividing it into 21 "bioregions." In turn, each of the 21 bioregions were divided into three zones:

1.   Wilderness area, designated as habitat of plants and animals, human habitation and use or intrusion is forbidden.
2.   Buffer zones surrounding the wilderness areas. Limited, and strictly controlled, human access is permitted within this zone.
3.   Cooperation zones, the only zones where humans are permitted to live.

According to the late Dr. Michael Coffman, of Environmental Perspectives, Inc., the strategy to implement such reserves and corridors would include:

» Start with a seemingly innocent-sounding program like the "World Heritage Areas in Danger." For example: Bring all human activity under regulation in a 14-18 million acre buffer zone around Yellowstone National Park.
» Next, declare all federal land (except Indian reservations) as buffers, along with private land that is within federal administration boundaries.
» Next, extend the U.S. Heritage corridor buffer zone concept along major river systems. Begin to convert critical federal lands and ecosystems to reserves.

» Finally, convert all U.S. Forest Service, grasslands, and wildlife refuges to reserves. Add missing reserves and corridors so that 50 percent of landscape is preserved.

» Each of the 21 bioregions will be governed by a bioregional council.

» "When the councils come into play, local, state, and national government will not be able to interfere with their governance. It will be under the strong arm of the UN Environmental organizations such as the Sierra Club, Nature Conservancy or other Green organizations which will be given the green light [to be] the enforcement arm of these councils at the local level." (Karen Lee Bixman, "The Taking of America")

Reed Noss summed it all up when he said, "the collective needs of non-human species must take precedence over the needs and desires of humans."

Next, the Wildlands Project became the basis for the UN's Convention on Biodiversity, which was also introduced at the 1992 Earth Summit along with Agenda 21. One plan laid down the blueprint for the reorganization of human society. The other detailed how that would be done. The UN's Biodiversity Assessment Report spelled it out pretty clearly when it defined what human activities would NOT be considered sustainable, so regulations would be needed to eliminate such practices. The targeted activities would include, "ski runs, grazing of live stock, plowing of soil, dust, building fences, industry, single family homes, paved and tarred roads, logging activities, and reservoirs, power line construction, and economic systems that fail to set proper values on the environment." Of course the evil economic system is free enterprise.

If fully implemented, the Convention on Biological Diversity would displace millions of people through massive regulations, nationalization of private land, and forcing people to move out of Core reserve areas and inner buffer zones. It would seriously reduce the production of agriculture, forest, and mining products. In the process, millions of Americans would lose their jobs. The resulting scarcity of resources would force Americans to pay double and triple for these products, including food and shelter. That result, of course, fits right in with the plan, forcing people to live on less -- the very root of the Sustainable Development scheme. So, finally, the ravings of a radical extremist, Dave Foreman, had become the basis for international law.

Even though Dr. Coffman, and the late Henry Lamb, two of the foremost experts on the rise of global governance, had succeeded in stopping the US Senate from ratifying the Biodiversity Treaty, parts of that plan were still implemented by breaking it down into a wide variety of programs, particularly through Bill Clinton's President's Council on Sustainable Development. There, just as Foreman envisioned, the Biodiversity plan along with Agenda 21, were divided into separate programs for nearly every agency of the federal government, as tools to successfully lock away vast areas of the nation and implemented through these agencies and state and local governments.

But how do you remove people from the land? One step at a time. There are many tools in place to stop human activity and expand the wilderness areas. Thomas Lovejoy, a science advisor to the federal Department of Interior said, "We will map the whole nation... determine development for the whole country, and regulate it." How?

» Deny grazing and water rights on public lands. It becomes more difficult and more expensive to run the farm or ranch – eventually the farmer goes out of business.
» Lock away natural resources by creating more national parks. It shuts down the mines – and they go out of business.
» Call every mosquito-infested swamp and occasional mud puddle a wetlands, and ban any development around it.
» Invent a Spotted Owl shortage and pretend it can't live in a forest where timber is cut. Shut off the forest. When no trees are cut, and there's nothing to feed the mills, then there are no jobs, and – they go out of business.

Several states have put together comprehensive plans to lock away massive amounts of state land from development. One effective tool is the banning of septic tanks in rural areas, making it impossible to live there. The only alternative, then, is to move into the cities.

Today the Wildlands Project comes under many names and many programs. Wilderness areas, Comprehensive land-use plans, Bikeways, Greenways, Heritage areas, land management, wetlands regulations, rails-to-trails, open space, wolf and bear reintroduction, Conservation Easements, and many more.

Each of these programs is designed to make it just a little harder to live on the land, a little more expensive, a little more hopeless. In reality the process is simply herding people off rural land and into human habitat areas – i.e., cities.

Following are just a few examples of the many programs being implemented in every part of the nation. New programs spring up every day, each with the same goal – control the land and the people in the name of Sustainable Development.

CHAPTER THIRTEEN

TOOLS FOR THE TRANSITION
FIRST, CONTROL THE WATER
IN THE RURAL AREAS

Control the water and you control life. Without water there can be no homes, towns, farming, or industry. If your goal is to change human society and dictate how it's to be developed, then controlling every aspect of how water can be used becomes the number one tool to achieve that end.

In 1972, the U.S. Congress passed the Clean Water Act. Its stated goal was to regulate discharges into the waters of the United States and control the quality of standards for surface waters. The federal Environmental Protection Agency (EPA) was put in charge of implementing the policy. It quickly created pollution control programs, surface water quality standards, and wastewater standards for industry.

Though the cause sounded noble (we all want clean air and water) the EPA, armed with the storm troopers of the NGOs, quickly turned the Act into a sledgehammer for enforcing Sustainable Development, usurping private property and controlling industry, even restricting the management practices of farms and ranches, down to the type of seeds they could use, and plants they could grow.

Permits, fees, and fines became the order of the day for nearly every action involving safe drinking water, industrial waste treatment, and ground water "protection." If the federal and state laws emanating from the Clean Air Act didn't go far enough to stop manufacturing and farming, the NGOs filled the void. They found a bonanza of free money for themselves by filing lawsuits against the federal government, charging it with not having enough laws! Eventually the EPA and other agencies became willing partners in such suits. If Congress didn't pass strict enough regulations, then the EPA actually encouraged their NGO partners to file suit against the EPA. When the suit was settled (they never made it into court, so there was no paper trail thus we have no idea of the facts – if any – established), the NGOs, not only got a nice settlement check, but also got their legal fees paid out of the settlement. And the EPA got more power. A win-win situation if there ever was one.

Over the years the power of the EPA and other regulatory agencies grew to a point of controlling nearly every action taken by industry, ranchers, farmers, and homeowners in the name of environmental protection. As its power to regulate grew, the EPA expanded its reach to include development along coastal shorelines, affecting private residences and communities located along them. Watersheds were designated, affecting water usage from the beginning springs, through creeks and small streams, to their meeting points into larger rivers, until they emptied into the oceans. In this way, the EPA, for example, could claim that farmers planting crops in the mountains of Cumberland, Maryland, directly affected the Chesapeake Bay, hundreds of miles away. That opened the way for tight controls of every human activity coming close to any of those sources of water that eventually feed into it.

AMERICAN HERITAGE RIVERS INITIATIVE

In 1997, President Bill Clinton issued Executive Order 13061 to establish the American Heritage Rivers Initiative (AHRI), claiming three objectives: natural resource and environmental protection, economic revitalization, and historic and cultural preservation. The White House sold the idea as a means to revitalize community waterfronts, preserve local history and, of course, protect the environment. It was all done, went the usual excuse, so the people could enjoy their rivers. Its true achievement was the establishment of a significant number of federal grants to be used by NGO groups to help the federal government institute means to regulate the country's waterways and any future development along them.

The late Congresswoman from Idaho, Helen Chenoweth, recognized the danger of the AHRI when she addressed Congress saying, "Mr. Speaker, I rise to alert my colleagues, and inform our constituents of the most recent assault by the Clinton Administration on private property rights, states rights, and western values – and that is the American Heritage Rivers Initiative, created and tendered solely by the White House and executed without congressional approval."

Because AHRI wasn't passed by Congress (and it was a federal edict not regulated by Congress), any group or individual could nominate a river to be an American Heritage river. And while rivers cross state boundaries, yet are not fully contained in one state, the Executive Order allowed for the successful circumventing of state legislatures. Without legislative approval, the affected portion of state or private land along the river would then come under the jurisdiction of the "river community," an undefined entity created in the Executive Order with no built-in limits to the size of the river areas in question. The initiative required partnership agreements between the federal government and local, regional governments, and the river community. In other words a federal agency would now control all decisions over the use of the river. Local control was lost. Of course, the initiative also implemented Sustainable Development.

Congresswoman Helen Chenoweth argued before Congress that the code of her state of Idaho states, "All waters of the state when flowing in their natural channels, including the waters of all natural springs and lakes within the boundaries of the states are declared to be the property of the state, whose duty it shall be to supervise their appropriation and allotment. Mr. Speaker, how can the Clinton Administration assert control over something it clearly does not own and (which) is so important to our state?"

Congress took no successful action to stop the American Heritage Rivers Initiative, and consequently, the structure of government was quietly changed from local representative and the will of the people to top down control by edict. Another step of Sustainable Development's drive for total control through regionalism was achieved.

WATERS OF THE US (WOTUS)

Barack Obama's EPA began pushing for more power through a new rule it called Waters of the US, or WOTUS and was intended to be part of its enforcement of the Clean Water Act but, instead, it drastically expand the EPA's authority to regulate both water and land.

Obama had already used the EPA as a major weapon in the establishment and enforcement of Sustainable Development. During his Administration, the EPA had added over 1,920 new regulations, most of which created few health or environmental benefits to the nation. Instead those regulations served to kill jobs and raise the costs of goods and services – all in the name of environmental protection, of course. The Heritage Foundation estimated that the EPA's twenty major rulemaking decisions (costing $100 million or more annually) could cost the United States over $36 billion per year.

Obama was pushing WOTUS which would give the federal government control of every drop of water in the nation. The greatest threat of WOTUS was its perversion of the definition of "navigable waters," based on the fact that water flows both above and below ground, all water was declared navigable because it would eventually end up, in theory, in a navigable collection of some sort. That interpretation gave the EPA the means to declare all water under their jurisdiction including that in ponds, drainage ditches, and other points of collection or flow. This made it a direct threat to private property as the EPA now declared dominion over all lands.

The Army Corps of Engineers has worked hand in glove with the EPA as another dangerous and determined arm of enforcement for such policies. For several decades the Corps has been arresting and prosecuting property owners for simply working their land.

In 2014, an Indiana farmer cleared trees from his property to expand his farmland. The Corps claimed that, by clearing his trees, the farmer had destroyed an ephemeral drainage. It was 118 miles away from traditional navigable waters. Navigable waters simply did not exist on the property before the trees were removed. The WOTUS would now support the Corps claim that a streambed existed where there was no evidence of it.

Worse, the Corps, in another case, asserted jurisdiction over a dirt road that had ruts which had collected rainwater. The Corps determined the ruts were a wetland.

The abuses by means of WOTUS were not the beginning of such outrageous government actions. It's been going on for several decades with a long list of victims, some still sitting in jail, others having their lives ruined and property lost simply for using their private property as owners have for centuries before the Sustainable onslaught began. Here are just a few of the cases.

John Pozsgai escaped communism in his native country of Hungry and settled in the township of Morrisville, Pennsylvania, but he didn't escape government tyranny. In 1990 he found himself in federal prison, serving a three-year sentence, not because he had committed robbery, or a violent act. John Pozsgai had violated the Clean Water Act.

Excited to finally be living in a free country, in 1986, he started to reach for the American dream. He purchased property with the intention of erecting a twelve thousand five hundred square-foot building to house his truck repair business to serve the community.

It so happened that the property he purchased was the site of an illegal dump, filled with old tires. Not only was the dump an eyesore, but more than 5,000 abandoned and rotting tires were blocking a storm water drainage ditch that had been installed by the county in 1936. The blocking of the drainage ditch has caused regular flooding of John's newly purchased land so he removed the tires and other trash that had been dumped there illegally over all of those years.

However, within months of that removal the Army Corps of Engineers sent notice that the land was a wetland, stemming from a "stream" that was connected to navigable waterways of the United States. There was no stream and there were no wetlands connected to the property, just the flooding caused by the illegal blockage of the drainage ditch that John Pozsgai had cleared.

When government agents came to the property to collect evidence for their accusations, Pozsgai, a man who believed his property was his own, told them to get off his land. The Army Corps sued him, then referred his case to the EPA, who then referred it to the Department of Justice for criminal prosecution.

The Army Corps of Engineers sued to force him to restore the property to its previous condition. In other words – put back the illegal dump – or at least its blockage of the drainage ditch. He did everything he possibly could to comply with the law and satisfy its orders, including obtaining a water quality permit from the state of Pennsylvania, even though the state had assured him that the land was not on the registry of wetlands.

In the end, John Pozsgai was arrested for cleaning up a thirty-year old illegal dump which should have been considered an environmental hazard. Instead of being rewarded for his heroic improvement of the environment he was sentenced to three years in prison and fined $202,000. The family finances were destroyed. John served a year and a half in prison, then spent an additional year and a half in a halfway house. Finally he was given five years supervised probation. At the time he was labeled the "worst environmental violator" in the history of the United States.

Serving his time for a non-crime didn't end his troubles. In 2002, three environmental organizations went to federal court, asking for the right to take Pozsgai to trial to force him to "restore" the site. These groups declared that the government had been too easy on him. Remember, the goal of the forces of Sustainable Development is to reorganize human society. Law, justice, truth, and reason just get in the way.

CHAPTER FOURTEEN

THEN...CONTROL THE LAND
THE ENDANGERED SPECIES ACT
IN THE RURAL AREAS

In 1973, the Endangered Species Act (ESA) was signed into law by President Richard Nixon. Its announced purpose was to protect and help recover species that were disappearing from the earth. Whales, polar bears, wolves, grizzly bears and bald eagles, were some of the most highly publicized species in need of rescue.

As a tool for "recovering" endangered species the ESA has been a monumental failure. In its thirty-year history, of the 1304 species that have been listed to save, only 12 have been officially recovered. That's a success rate of only 1%. Why? What went wrong?

Answer – the ESA was created as a tool to take and control private land, not recover species. In fact, once a species has been listed no recovery plan is ever required. If that seems strange concerning an act that is so highly touted as a major plan to protect wildlife, then one must remember the true purpose of Sustainable Development. Again, it is not an environmental plan, but a diabolical policy to reorganize and control human civilization.

Here's how the ESA really works. With pressure from NGO groups, the federal government declares that a certain species is endangered so the species is placed on the ESA list. Now, if that endangered species is discovered on a farm or a ranch – or in the middle of a proposed building project, all human action on the affected property is stopped. No ranching, no farming, no drilling, no timber or mining activity, and no building may take place. Essentially the land is rendered worthless and locked away. Understand that 90% of all species (endangered or otherwise) claim habitation on private land, so the ESA becomes the perfect tool if your goal is to lock away land and stop industry. Not much good, however, for the animals.

Punishment of the landowner is the direct effect of the ESA. It's interesting to consider that if an endangered species is found on a property, perhaps it's because the landowner has actually been doing something right to encourage and provide the proper habitat. Such thoughts are never considered by government agents and their Green stormtroopers. The result has been that any landowner who discovers the existence of an endangered specie on his land quickly understands that, in order to keep it, he needs to adopt the SSS policy -- shoot, shovel and shut up! Get rid of the foul creature and say nothing of its existence – or lose your land and go to jail. Not a very effective atmosphere for trying to save wildlife, but sometimes the only way to save a person's property.

Yet every attempt to fix the deadly punitive affects of the ESA has been refused by the environmentalists. They will not hear of changing a single comma in the ESA. Again, saving species is not the purpose. Land control is the goal. Facts about whether listed species are really endangered simply get in the way.

THE SPOTTED OWL

Two decades ago, the nation was warned that spotted owls were disappearing because big bad timber companies were cutting down "old growth" forests. Old growth is an invented term to define forests that have not yet been harvested by the timber industry.

So the Sustainablists rushed to the forests, hugged the trees, and issued news releases to decry the evils of the logging industry. Save the owl! Save the trees! Kill the timber industry! Of course, that was the point. As a result of the hysteria to save the "endangered" owls, U.S. timber sales were reduced by 80-90%, forcing sawmills to close, loggers to go broke, and whole towns, which depended on the industry, to die. The federal crackdown on the industry caused a shift from U.S. domestic lumber purchases to those from foreign soils. In short, American industry suffered in the name of protecting the spotted owl. Turns out it wasn't endangered.

First, the spotted owl is a sub-species of the Mexican spotted owl. There are lots of them! Second, it wasn't the timber industry driving down the spotted owl populations – it was the completely natural consequence of competition with another species of owl – the barred owl.

Third, the spotted owl didn't have to have "old growth forests" to live. They were found living (and procreating) in McDonald signs, under bridges, and many other places. Another Green lie that accomplished the desired and pre-determined outcome – death to the timber industry – all in the name of environmental protection.

POLAR BEARS

The next frantic endangered species crisis was the dying population of polar bears – all because of man's encroachment on their northern habitat as well as the evil drillers of oil in the arctic. To this day, the World Wildlife Fund continues to run dramatic, heart rendering ads on television, showing drowning polar bears clinging to life as they cling to a melting hunk of ice.

Oh the tragedy. Immediately, Congress rushed to the rescue as Representative Ed Markey, Chairman of the House Select Committee on Energy Independence and Global Warming, issued legislation to stop drilling rights in the Chukchi Sea. He said this area of drilling "may be" needed as critical habitat for the polar bears' survival. Of course, Global Warming was to blame for the melting ice. Another man-made assault on nature.

Again, it was all a lie. According to the National Oceanic and Atmospheric Administration (NOAA) average Alaskan temperatures were NOT climbing. The ice was not melting. Today, it is at an all time high thickness.

Most importantly, polar bear populations are not declining. They are growing. The total population in the area was about 22,000 bears. Now, according to the Canadian government, local hunts are necessary to keep the populations under control.

WOLF REINTRODUCTION

For several hundred years our ancestors worked diligently to remove predators from the land so they could live in peace, without fear for their children and livestock. Over the past several decades, the forces of Sustainable Development have demanded that government enforce policy to bring back the wolves and grizzly bears that ranchers and farmers had fought so hard to keep at a viable but controlled number.

When the people protested, saying the wolves and grizzles would destroy their lives and livelihood, the Greens insisted man could live in harmony with these predators because there had never been a case of wolves killing humans. Moreover, they argued that the wolves would be good for the elk populations and that the wolves only kill what they need to eat. The government, of course, acceded to the Greens' demands and brought the wolves and bears back as protected species.

So, wolves were dropped on the plains of Montana, Idaho, and other western states. Then reality set in. With no predators of their own, the packs of wolves grew rapidly, reproducing at a rapid rate. Over 2,000 wolves caused 45% of known deaths of radio-collared female elk on the northern ridge of Montana. Elk populations decreased from 16,791 in 1995 to 8,335 in 2004, doubling the rate of kills predicted by the ESA. In addition, contrary to the noble narrative of wolves killing only what they needed to eat, it was discovered that they actually will eat their prey while it's still alive, sometimes eating only a portion and leaving the prey to suffer as they die slowly. Wolves, it was discovered, were actually treacherous and not to be trusted.

How would you feel if this was YOUR best friend?

Humans soon became the prey. Hunters reported being surrounded by packs of wolves, cleverly hunting them like a scene from Jurassic Park. One resident in Idaho reported a pack of wolves sitting in her yard as she walked down her driveway. As she tried to call a neighbor for help, they surrounded her, closing in, almost upon her before help finally arrived.

In New Mexico, two school children were followed home from the bus stop by three wolves. In Idaho a wolf kill was found 70 yards from a school bus stop. Yet the wolves are the ones our own government chooses to protect, not our children.

Meanwhile, wolves routinely attack and kill pets and livestock, just as predicted by the ranchers and farmers. The Sustainable movement is based on anti-human policy, perpetrated by deceit and promoted by myth as it drives its plan to destroy human society. Yet it's hard for most humans to comprehend that other humans want to rid most of us from the earth.

HIDING THE SLAUGHTER CAUSED BY THE WINDMILLS

If you are caught simply carrying the feather of an endangered eagle it could lead to huge fines and even imprisonment. They are sacred and not to be messed with – according to accepted environmental lore.

Of course, it's also accepted lore that wind power is natural and therefore sacred. Wind energy advocates insist that those gigantic turbines, which now cover vast acres of the nation, "only" kill an "acceptable" number of birds, perhaps 440,000 annually.

That is hundreds of times more than were killed in the Exxon Valdez or BP Gulf of Mexico oil spills. It's also 1,900 times more dead birds than the 2011 case which prompted the U.S. Justice Department and Fish and Wildlife Service to prosecute oil companies operating in North Dakota in 2011.

The "acceptable" kill rate by wind turbines is also pure fabrication of numbers, aided and abetted by the same government officials and Sustainablists who never miss an the opportunity to pillory and prosecute oil producers. The actual death toll from wind turbine blades is an intolerable and unsustainable 13,000,000 to 39,000,000 birds and bats annually, year after year, in the United States alone. And the number grows with the increase of new turbines. But don't worry, those kills are acceptable because wind power is environmentally and politically correct!

CHAPTER FIFTEEN

CONSERVATION EASEMENTS AND THEIR THREAT TO PROPERTY OWNERS
IN THE RURAL AREAS

The Green Mafia tells us conservation easements are the only way to save the family farm. Without the tax credits and restrictions on development rights, America will be paved over and Astroturf will replace sod. We're in a crisis, they tell us. However, as H.L. Mencken once warned, "A plan to save humanity is almost always a false front for the urge to rule."

There's no question that the family farm is under assault. Rising taxes, international trade agreements that subsidize foreign markets to dump their goods, inflation, and government regulations are all eating away at the ability to keep the farm operating. Now add uncontrollable issues like weather conditions and market fluctuations. Few other businesses face such overwhelming odds for success. Yet rarely does one meet a farmer who wants to give up and stop working the land that often his ancestors first acquired. In most cases it's agony for a farmer to decide to sell his property. On the other hand, the land is his main asset. To provide a good life for the family, selling the land, many times to developers, maybe necessary for survival.

However, there is now a much more lethal threat facing small farmers and the outrageousness of it is that this threat is being disguised as a way to help them. The real threat is the green solution - "Conservation Easements." And farmers are being sucked into the trap all across the country.

Conservation easements are promoted by land trusts and environmental groups. Tax breaks are granted. Even cash is offered those farmers willing to sell their development rights, under the argument that this will drive away the temptation to sell the land to nasty developers, thus keeping it farmland. The clever slogan, "farm land lost is farm land lost forever" helps sell the case for easements.

The promoters of such ideas are very good with the sales pitch. If it were politically correct to do so, one could actually hear patriotic music playing in the background as the promises to save the family farm roll off the pitchman's tongue.

Say proponents, "A conservation easement is a voluntary perpetual agreement that restricts non-agricultural uses such as mining and large scale residential and commercial development." They boldly promote the easements by promising that "the landowner continues to own, live on, and use the land." They even promise that the land can be passed down to heirs, along with generous tax credits. What's not to like? Desperate farmers are flocking to the pitchman's wagon to buy his life-saving potion.

Of course, as another famous pitchman, P.T. Barnum, once said, "there's a sucker born every minute." Farmers beware the slick talker who has the answers to your woes. His answers may well be your demise – and your farm's. It's wise to read the fine print of a conservation easement agreement. Here are some facts.

The first thing that every landowner should know about conservation easements is who are the true forces behind them, and what is their real purpose? Conservation easements are, in fact, a cleverly disguised piece of the Wildlands Project. Conservation easements and the purchasing of development rights are key to the basic Wildlands concept of connecting corridors of wilderness areas. Dave Foreman gave away the plot when he said, "If we identify a ranch ... that's between two wilderness reserves, and we feel it will be necessary as a corridor, we can say to the rancher, 'We don't want you to give up your ranch now, but let us put a conservation easement on it. Let's work out the tax details so you can donate it in your will to this reserve system."

Once the landowner has signed the agreement, the deed is done and the trap is shut. The easement agreements are almost always "in perpetuity," meaning FOREVER. There is no way out. Even if your children later inherit the land and choose to use it for their own purposes, it can never be undone. They are stuck with a piece of property that has no value to them and basically the only people interested in purchasing the land would be the land trust – for a greatly reduced price, of course, if you weren't also forced to "leave" the land to the trust in the easement contract.

Again, those determined to rule the world leave no stone unturned in their drive for control. They are creative in their pursuit. They are ruthless in their drive. They are diabolical.

THE FACTS ABOUT CONSERVATION EASEMENTS

In a typical conservation easement, a private land trust organization purchases some or all of the "bundle" of a property owner's rights. The bundle includes an agreement to give up development rights for the property; the ability to overrule the owner's choice of how to use the property, including adding more buildings or renovating or rebuilding existing buildings; in the case of farmers, it may include decisions on which fields can be uses for planting or even which crops can be grown and the technique to be used. All of these things come under the command of the easement. And all of it may become the decision of the land trust, because, once the conservation easement agreement is signed, the owner's rights are legally subservient to his new partner, the trust.

True, in exchange, the property owner receives charitable deductions on federal taxes based on the difference between the values of the land before and after granting the easement. The property owner also receives relief from federal estate or inheritance taxes. Many states provide income tax credits and property tax relief. And the owner receives a payment for his development rights.

In the beginning it all sounds good. Money in the pocket; the farm safe from development and the ability to practice the beloved tradition of farming. Well, maybe.

The fact is, under the easement, the owner has sold away his property rights and therefore no longer has controlling interest in his property. Through the restrictions outlined in the easement, property usage is now strictly controlled, including everyday decisions on running the farm. In many cases, the Land Trust that controls the easement demands strict adherence to "sustainable" farming practices. That means strict controls on how much energy or water can be used in the farming process, access to streams for the livestock, use of fertilizer, etc, are all under the direction of the Land Trust. And there's more. Certain details weren't revealed to the landowner as he signed on the dotted line. For example:

» Trusts often re-sell the easement to other conservation groups. They sell and resell them like commodities. Eventually the farmer may not know who actually holds the control over his land. For these groups, the easements become a significant profit center as they rake in fees for each new easement they sign up.

» Worse, the land trust may work directly with government agencies, helping to establish new regulations which alter best management practices, driving up compliance costs. Eventually these cost increases can force owners into a desperate situation and they are more than ready to sell the land.

» In certain targeted areas where the land trusts are especially interested in locking away the land, owners who refuse to sign an easement may find themselves under massive pressure to do so. The Nature Conservancy is a master at this trick, creating millions of dollars of income for the group. Its favorite practice is to tell the landowner that the government intends to take the land, but, if they sell to the Conservancy, it will guarantee that the land will stay in private hands, but of course, since the government intends to take the land it is now worth much less. So they get the landowner to sell at a reduced rate. Then the Conservancy calls the government agency to tell them the good news that they have the land. And the agency pays the Conservancy full market value. They call that, "Capitalism with a heart!!"

» Because ownership rights are muddled between taxes, restrictions, and best practices requirements, it can be difficult to find a buyer willing to pay a fair market price for the land. In a sense, once the easement is signed, the owner has just rendered his land worthless on the open market.

» Conservation easement deeds use broad language that expands the trust's control but very specific language that limits the landowner's rights.

» When productive land is taken off the local tax rolls, a revenue shortage is created that has to be made up by other taxpayers, causing rate hikes in property taxes and other tricks the government can come up with to keep the same amount of money coming in even though thousands of acres are being taken off the tax rolls.

At a January, 2013, meeting of the Fauquier County, Virginia planning commission, it was revealed that 96,600 acres of county land is in conservation easements (or 23% of the total land mass of the county). A little research revealed an interesting detail. It seems that, as the conservation easements are sold to the public as a way to save the small family farm, in reality, of the 23% of the land in easements, only 2% of it is actually small family farms. The rest is basically the vast estates of the landed gentry who have found a way to not only keep the land open for their fox hunts – but to also reduce their property taxes.

10 QUESTIONS TO ASK BEFORE SIGNING A CONSERVATION EASEMENT

Are You Asking the Right Questions about Conservation Easements or Purchased Development Rights?

Special thanks to Ric Frost – Economic Policy Analyst

Many landowners have placed portions, or all, of their private land holdings into a split estate situation without fully understanding the impacts to themselves, or their community. This is largely due to not asking enough questions, or the right questions.

1. **Why would someone want to pay to control my land, and where is the money coming from?**

2. **I have signed away my rights, but can the Land Trust transfer their rights?**

3. **What will my kids have left if I do this?**

4. **Do Conservation Easements protect agriculturalists from the real pressures of ownership, as is claimed by land trusts? These pressures would include:**

Government restrictions and regulations that affect farming;

» Tax Exempt, Non-Government Environmental Organization Lawsuits against property owners;
» Weather Fluctuations;
» Market Fluctuations;
» Protection for farmers market pricing structures (or the ability to pass on increased business costs, such as fuel expenses);
» Protection from Subsidized Foreign Market Dumping.

» Protection from Estate Taxes and compliance costs.

These are the real reasons farmers can't stay in business and are forced to sell their land – not pressure from developers.

Here's the answer to that question -- Conservation Easements DO NOT protect farmers from these pressures.

5. If land trusts are concerned with protecting agriculture, then what have they done to alleviate these real pressures?

Splitting the title of private land through Conservation Easements has other consequences as well. Some comments on CE and PDR impacts by financial officers:

> "Owners give up management and control of the land": Jimmy Hall, PCA, NM
> "Severely diminished loan value of land": John Johnson, First Western Bank, SD
> "CEs eliminate property loan value": Dee Gidney, Texas Bank Ag Loans, TX
> "Fragmentation of land title to deny future generations a full range of productive land-use options": David Guernsey, Alliance for America
> Loan Value for operational and other loans is reduced up to 90 percent with an Easement

6. What are the real facts vs the misguided sales pitches?

» "Perpetual means 99 years." False: PERPETUAL is FOREVER.
» "I retain full title to the land." False: title becomes split with easement holder.
» "A CE (PDR) is the only way the land is managed to my intent." False: the easement holder and future easement holder (LAND TRUSTS) can change management practices at any time, including development! Easement management loopholes also allow easement holders and third party non-easement holder interests to sue the landowner (not the easement holder trust) and impose habitat restrictions.
» "A CE (PDR) allows me to use the property as I always have had." False: you give up management control of all easement property forever!

» "Property with a CE (PDR) will sell easy." False: a CE (PDR) may reduce the property value, and affect the willingness of financial institutions to loan money on a split title.

7. **Questions landowners and local governments should ask before accepting or promoting Conservation Easements:**

» What could be unexpected economic impacts that may be encountered as the result of Conservation Easements and Property Development Rights? Some of the impacts already experienced by landowners and communities have been:

» Reduced management options on taxed lands of landowner and heirs,

» Restrictions on farm and ranch management practices, Restrictions on chemicals used, Restrictions on seed and plant types, Restrictions on farm and ranch management practices,

» Reduction of income due to restrictions,

» Reduction in management options with land and business value decline, forcing owner into a "willing seller" status (actually a compromised seller),

» Imposition of Environmental Assessment (EA) and Environmental Impact Study (EIS) expenses on landowner for management changes, especially if a Federal Nexus exists,

» Legal expenses incurred by the Land Trust for enforcement and penalty expenses for CE and PDR violations (It's built into the fine print),

» Vulnerability from non-trust third party interest lawsuits – Litigation Exposure is in the Easement Act,

» Decreased or eliminated production translating into negative economic impacts to agriculture and related industries within community, county, and state.

» Recent reports indicate a majority of lands with CEs (PDRs) have not remained in agriculture, and are rendered to untaxed "open space" in the hands of the government, or owned by wealthy non-agriculturalists comfortable with "open space" restricted lands without production,

» Reduced Management Options on taxed lands of landowner and heirs,

» Reduction of income due to restrictions of direct, induced, and indirect economic benefits to all related industries within community, county and state,

» Reduction of county tax base forcing tax increases and reduction of county services on other property owners to make up the loss (a disproportionate burden).

8. **Questions that landowners, who are approached for CEs or PDRs, should ask are:**

» What are CE (PDR) impacts to private landowners and communities?

» Do the "benefits" offset the impacts? (Lost tax revenue and future earnings opportunities)

» What are the other impacts and implications from imposing a CE (PDR) on private land? (Federal Nexus and Section 7)

» What is the long-range outcome from imposing a CE (PDR) on private landowners?

According to whom? (A tax-exempt organization?)

Would a limited liability company or incorporation better serve the landowner's tax needs, instead of a CE (PDR) that brings in tax-exempt third party litigation and potential federal agency management?

9. **Would it not be better to protect agriculture by:**

» Supporting reduced environmental restrictions on agricultural producers?

» Stopping the dumping of foreign commodities on our markets by foreign subsidized products, at prices lower than producers' cost of operation?

» Making agriculture attractive as a viable business career and encouraging our youth to remain in agriculture as a productive and fulfilling life?

10. **Questions that State and County officials should be considering for CE and PDR regulations are:**

» License and regulate land trust agents as real estate agents.

» Regulation of tax-exempt land trusts by state real estate commission (they are acting as land brokers).

» Bonding requirement on each CE and PDR transaction equivalent to value of encumbered property before transaction.

» Renegotiation language built into CE contract that allows grantee to renegotiate every 5 Years (North Dakota has 10 year limits – no perpetuity allowed!).

» If renegotiations cannot be accomplished to satisfaction of landowner, the CE contract becomes null and void.

» Land Trust pays back-taxes on land if this occurs, not landowner (don't forget that if a CE or PDR is ended, under current IRS law the landowner pays the IRS the back-taxes back to the time of the origin of the CE or PDR, not the tax-exempt land trust).

» Land trust pays taxable value of severed development right to county to prevent erosion of tax base as community infrastructure demands increase (check with county appraiser for development right tax values).

» No CE shall be valid and enforceable unless the limitations or obligations created by the easement are clearly presented in writing on the face of any document creating the CE or PDR Including Information From the UCEA 1981 (Uniform Conservation Easement Act).

» Water, grazing, farming and mineral rights shall not be encumbered by conditions or restrictions imposed or agreed to in the CE or PDR Contract. Grantee (landowner) retains rights of transfer on all rights not expressly identified in CE or PDR.

» Local and state legislation expressly prohibiting transfer of CE or PDR to other parties without formal written consent of landowner (a common practice of land trusts is to trade CEs and PDRs without knowledge or consent of landowner).

» Elimination of third-party enforcement clause language from CE contracts – must be state law! (Colorado has this law, and it has been upheld in at least one case).

Remember, restricting land through Conservation Easements or Purchased Development Rights in the name of "protecting agriculture" simply put, does not protect agriculture!

Perhaps the simplest way to end the tyranny of conservation easements over the landowners is for state government to allow a five year opt out of the conservation easement for the landowner. This would allow enough time for them to decide if the easement is working for them.

And what about the tax credits they have already received? Simple. They received them while under the easement. They stop receiving the tax credits when they opt out. No muss. No fuss.

Better yet, stop the massive taxes and regulations and let the landowners use their property as they wish. Of course that would be contrary to the agenda for reorganization of human society.

Conservation easements are not a tool for property owners to preserve their land. All the tax breaks and rhetoric about helping farmers is just that – rhetoric for the specific purpose of pressuring the owner to give up control of the land. In truth, the creation of the conservation easement ruse is a brilliant tactic by the Sustainable Development forces to get landowners to give up their property rights voluntarily.

CHAPTER SIXTEEN

NATIONAL HERITAGE AREAS ASSAULT ON PRIVATE PROPERTY AND LOCAL COMMUNITY RULE

Preserving history! How much more American can you get? The major opponents of the Sustainable power grab are the folks who love our nation, revere our Constitution and will do almost anything to preserve the ideals that created our beloved nation. Visiting historic areas, walking the hallowed ground of our battlefields, learning the details of the Founders' every thought and action, these are the things that set the passions of America's patriots on fire. These are the people who would oppose any action that would violate the Constitution or infringe on private property rights as they defend free enterprise every step of the way. They are the greatest opponents of Sustainable Development's drive for an all-powerful central government.

How do the power mongers guide such opponents into their trap? Answer! Historic Preservation! There are a lot of programs popping out of the federal government under the name of historic preservation. It's interesting to note how many have come about since the drive began to impose Sustainable Development. There are Scenic Rivers designations. We've already discussed the American Heritage Rivers Initiative. Of course there's the National Register of Historic Places and the National Historic Landmarks Program, to name just a few.

Then there are National Heritage Areas. Heritage areas are sold as a means to honor historic or cultural events that took place in a specific locale. We are told that they will preserve our culture and honor the past, that they will preserve battlefields where our forefathers fought and died for freedom, and they will preserve birthplaces, homes, buildings and hallowed grounds for posterity. Of course, we are assured that Heritage Areas will also help build tourism and boost local economies.

What is a National Heritage Area? To put it bluntly, it is a pork barrel earmark that harms property rights and local governance. Why is that true? Because Heritage Areas have boundaries. These are very defined boundaries with very definite consequences for folks who reside within them. National historic significance, obviously, is a very arbitrary term; so anyone's property can end up falling under those guidelines.

Here are the details as to how a Heritage Area operates. Specifically, funding and technical assistance for Heritages Areas are administered through the National Park Service, a federal agency with a long history of hostility toward private landowners.

The recipient of these funds, in partnership with the Park Service, become a "managing entity" for the activities and development of the Heritage Area. Who are the recipients of these funds? As usual, they are typically strictly ideological special interests groups and local government officials. The managing entity sets up non-elected boards, councils, and regional governments to oversee policy inside the Heritage Area. In other words, Heritage Areas are set up just like all Sustainable Development operations.

In the mix of special interest groups you're going to find all of the usual suspects: environmental groups, planning groups, historic preservation groups, all with their own private agendas – all working behind the scenes, creating policy, hovering over the members of the non-elected boards (even assuring that their own people make up the boards), and all collecting the Park Service funds to pressure local governments to install their agenda. In many cases, these groups actually form a compact with the Interior Department to determine the guidelines that make up the land-use management plan and the boundaries of the Heritage Area itself.

After the Heritage Area boundaries are drawn, and after the management plan has been approved by the Park Service, the management entity and its special interest groups are given the federal funds, typically a million dollars or more per year, and told to spend that money getting the management plan enacted at the local level.

Here's how they operate with those funds. They go to local boards and local elected officials and say, "Congress just created a new Heritage Area and you are within the boundaries. We have identified certain properties within these boundaries as those we deem significant. We have also identified certain businesses that we deem insignificant and harmful to these properties are harmful to the Heritage Area. We don't have the power to make laws to regulating control over these properties and businesses, but you do. And here is some federal money. Now use whatever tools, whatever laws, whatever regulatory procedures you already have to make this management plan come into fruition."

Incredibly, proponents argue that National Heritage Areas do not influence local zoning or land-use planning. Yet by definition this is precisely what they do. Found right in the language of Heritage Area legislation, the management entity is specifically directed to restore, preserve, and manage anything and everything that is naturally, culturally, historically, and recreationally significant to the Heritage Area.

This sweeping mandate ensures that virtually every square inch of land within the boundaries is subject to the scrutiny of Park Service bureaucrats and their managing partners. That is the way it works. It's done behind the scenes – out of the way of public input.

It is also worth noting that these are permanent units of the Park Service. Proponents claim NHAs are merely seed grants and that, sooner or later, they will attain self-sufficiency and no longer need federal funding. Yet National Heritage Areas almost never meet their funding sunset triggers. Once created, they are permanent units of the National Park Service and always dependent on increased federal funds. And the Park Service has testified several times that they, indeed, could be considered permanent units of the Park Service because they always need oversight.

In addition, within the Heritage Areas, the Park Service looks for opportunities to create other Park Service programs. Former Deputy Director of the National Park Service, Donald Murphy, testified before the Senate Subcommittee on National Parks that one of the things the Park Service does when administering National Heritage Areas is survey land that would be suitable for future National Parks or National Park expansions.

Of course, as with so many other invasive planning schemes, there is always the assurance that these are local initiatives, and that Heritage Areas are something citizens want in order to bring an honorary federal designation to help drive tourism into their regions.

It simply isn't true. For the most part, Heritage Areas are first dreamed up by national organizations or small wealthy organizations within the locality, which are looking to promote their own agendas – paid for by federal tax dollars. The process then becomes federally driven by the National Park Service, which uses the legislation to hand out cash to the very organizations that are pushing them.

THE CONNECTION BETWEEN HERITAGE AREAS AND SUSTAINABLE DEVELOPMENT

The language used in Congressional legislation (H.R. 4099, a bill from 2012, to "Authorize a National Heritage Area Program) has been very revealing. Describing the "need" for Heritage Areas, it said: "Certain areas of the United States tell nationally significant stories; they illustrate significant aspects of our heritage; possess exceptional natural, cultural, scenic, and historic resources; and represent the diversity of our national character."

Ok, so, name a section of our nation that doesn't contain "significant stories." Or locate a place where people from the past didn't walk, live, or carry on their lives. That definition is simply too broad to be practical, if the real purpose is to honor significant events in our history.

But the bill goes on to explain: "In these areas, the interaction of natural processes, geography, history, cultural traditions, and economic and social forces form distinctive landscapes that should be recognized, conserved, enhanced, and interpreted to improve the quality of life in the regions and to provide opportunities for public appreciation, education, enjoyment, and economic sustainability."

Where have we heard these very words before – economic and social forces; conserve; improve the quality of life?

Well, again, lets go back to this quote from the 1993 President's Council on Sustainable Development which said, "*Sustainable Communities encourage people to work together to create healthy communities where natural resources are preserved, jobs are available, sprawl is contained, neighborhoods are secure, education is lifelong, transportation and health care are accessible, and all citizens have opportunities to improve the quality of their lives.*"

We've already learned that the purpose of the President's Council on Sustainable Development was to create policy to reduce or eliminate "unsustainable" activities by controlling such things as consumerism, high meat intake, use of fossil fuels, roadways, automobiles, dams, pastures, golf courses, and much more.

So, now wait a minute. Are we talking about historic preservation where we just want to honor our past – or are we talking about a massive zoning process involving central planning? Because that's what Sustainable Development is. Even the planning groups will admit that. So, why is the same language of Sustainable Development in a bill on Heritage Areas? Could they possibly be part of the same top down agenda?

In that light, consider this additional quote from the President's Council: "Private land-use decisions are often driven by strong economic incentives that result in several ecological and aesthetic consequences... the key to overcoming it is through public policy." That means new legislation and government programs. And so, what are Heritage Areas but legislation for a new government program?

Did the people of the affected areas really ask for a Heritage Area or did this idea just appear for no apparent reason? Is there an emergency? Is there a dire need? If so, can anybody name those needs? These questions must be asked before such policy is put in place.

And finally, there is this quote from the same policy making source – the President's Council: "*We need a new collaborative decision process that leads to better decisions, more rapid change and more sensible use of human, natural and financial resources in achieving our goals.*" Better decisions for whom – by whom? More sensible use of resources, according to whom? Ask these same questions about any of the policies so far detailed in this report – from Conservation Easements, to American Heritage Rivers. Where is the urgency?

This description of government leads away from elected representatives doing the people's bidding. Instead it establishes non-elected boards, councils, and regional government entities in which local citizens have little or no input. The language is the same between Sustainable Development and Heritage Areas because they are both part of the same "collaborative" process and for the same purpose – control of the land and all human activity inside it.

As proponents talk about historic preservation and heritage inside the Heritage Area, you will also find the catchwords "resource conservation" and "resource stewardship," for example. It's all about control. Control of the land. Control of resources, Control of decision-making. And how does that fit with the claim of preserving the American culture - which was built on the ideals of free enterprise and private property? The fact is, it doesn't.

In reality, National Heritage Areas are nothing more than land targeted by the NPS for future national parks, historic sites, landmarks, and land acquisition for the specific purpose of limiting human activity – adding to the Wildlands.

Proponents of NHAs also claim that they are "locally driven" projects. Nothing could be further from the truth. Landowners within the boundaries of proposed Heritage Areas are left in the dark throughout the entire process. Why? Because each and every Heritage Area bill refuses to include simple written notification to property owners. Seemingly the Park Service and their management "partners" are not too eager to share all the good news with the local citizenry.

I have personally been in meetings with congressional staffers to discuss Heritage Areas, specifically the staff of former Congressman Frank Wolfe, a major proponent of Heritage Areas. I asked them if they intended to notify affected landowners living inside the boundaries of a specific Heritage Area. They looked at me like I had two heads. They shuffled their feet and looked down at the table and then said, "there's no way to do that." "It would be too costly." "How could we reach everyone?" And then they quickly moved to change the subject.

Of course the ability is there. The mailman delivers to each and every one of the homes in the designated area every day. The fact is, they don't want to tell residents in advance, they might object. And that would disrupt the "process." No matter how noble a project may sound, alarm bells should go off when proponents want to enforce their vision in secret.

If these National Heritage Areas were truly driven by local enthusiasm there would be no reason to keep the plans secret. Instead, local enthusiasm would have attracted and generated local funding to create local Heritage Areas. But, National Heritage Areas depend on federal tax dollars because they lack local interest, and not a single Heritage Area has ever succeeded in attracting that interest throughout their entire infinite lives.

The federal money is the villain. If local residents just wanted to honor an area for its historic or cultural achievements, a simple resolution from Congress and a plaque at the county line could do that. That alone would help bring in the promised tourism, of course, it's not about that. It's about money, control, and agendas.

There are currently 49 National Heritage Areas across the country so far. Here are just a few tidbits about them and how they operate:

» The entire city of Baltimore is a National Heritage Area.

» The entire State of Tennessee is covered by the Tennessee Civil War National Heritage Area.

» In Waterloo, Iowa, which is a major part of the nation's breadbasket and home of John Deer tractors, **Silos and Smoke Stacks Heritage Area** was sold as a means to "honor" the farmers. Since its creation, not much has changed for farmers inside the Heritage Area. There has been no focus by its leaders to actually help farmers by keeping taxes down or helping them compete with oversees competitors. Instead, they are essentially putting American farmland in a museum. But Waterloo's slumlords who owned dilapidated buildings and empty store fronts in the downtown area did receive massive taxpayer funding to fix up their buildings and raise their rents. There are strict controls on use of the buildings, including how they can be repaired or upgraded. Grants flow like water to special interests in the name of historic preservation. There are educational programs paid for by taxpayers for such vital subjects as why manure is important to farm life. And in the process, downtown Waterloo has been designated as an historic area. There's only one problem -- nothing much of historic significance actually happened in downtown Waterloo. As usual, follow the money.

» Along the Mississippi River there are two Heritage Areas, **Mississippi Delta National Heritage Area and Mississippi Gulf Coast National Heritage Area**. Now here is a region rich in history. There must be all kinds of good things happening along the mother of all rivers. Well, today you won't find people participating in one of the grand historic traditions of the river – living on riverboats. There were once whole generations of river people living on such boats. Talk about American Heritage – right out of Mark Twain. But, back in the 1990s, as part of Bill Clinton's American Heritage Rivers Initiative, those living on houseboats were moved off the river. Certain other boat traffic and river activities were also curtailed. It was all in the name of environmental protection, of course. In addition, the traditional flood plain designations were moved to an extreme distance from the river, making it impossible for existing homes to get flood insurance, and stopping any further building along the river. This was land-use planning – right out of the Sustainable Development plan and the Wildlands project. So, the Heritage Areas were used to honor what? Certainly not life on the river. They are essentially putting the Mississippi River in a museum.

» In West Virginia we find the National Coal Heritage Area. Introduced in 1996 by Congressman Rahall, it was sold as a way to honor the coal industry. Apparently, Rahall thought that since the miners have all lost their jobs to environmentalism, perhaps he can make up for it by throwing a few extra bucks their way to give tours of their bankrupt area. Take this challenge – just try to mine a lump of coal inside the

National Coal Heritage Area. Not on your life. Restricted. Taboo. In short, they have put West Virginia coal in a museum. Do you get the picture?

» **The Journey Through Hallowed Ground Heritage Area** created a 175- mile-long federal corridor, encompassing portions of Virginia, Maryland and Pennsylvania. Of course it was sold as a means to honor and protect some of the most precious historic areas of the nation, running from Jefferson's Monticello to the Gettysburg battlefield. The chief sponsor was Virginia Republican, Congressman Frank Wolfe, who promoted it saying, "The Journey Through Hallowed Ground Corridor holds more American history than any other region in the country and its recognition as a National Heritage Area will elevate its national prominence as deserved." He also claimed that it was an "effort to create economic opportunity by celebrating the unique place in American history the region holds." **There's one major problem with all of those promises. Every one of those designated sites are already preserved and are major tourist attractions.** The only difference is that now all of the homes, businesses and towns inside the borders of the Heritage Area are subjected to the control of the National Park Service. The legislation assigned the usual "management entity" consisting of the Journey Through Hallowed Ground Partnership. This was an umbrella group of preservation activists and lobbyists which helped move the legislation through Congress. They now stand to directly benefit from the power gained from the bills passage. Also strongly pushing for passage was the Department of Interior, which saw the Heritage Area as a means to oversee development and land-use in the area. An additional example of a group that pushed hard to establish the JTHG Heritage Area was the National Trust for Historic Preservation. Another was Scenic America.

These last two named are national groups that have very benign titles but very serious missions. But are they interested in just historic preservation or massive top-down controlled land-use restrictions?

Well, here is some insight into the answer to that question. You may have heard about Measure 37 in Oregon passed in 2004. This is a basic property rights initiative that isn't very hard to support no matter who you are, even if you are indifferent to property rights. All it does is reaffirm the Fifth Amendment to the Constitution. It simply says that when state or local governments pass laws that take away somebody's property rights and devalue their property, those states and local governments have to compensate that person, or if they can't compensate that person, they have to waive the regulation. It is that simple. It basically stops state and local governments from stealing private land.

It passed overwhelmingly despite a massive campaign by Greens to try to prevent it, and it was even upheld by the Oregon Supreme Court. And groups like the National Trust for Historic Preservation and Scenic America actually fought this ballot initiative tooth and nail. It had nothing to do with historic preservation *per se*, or a scenic America, but obviously these groups have a much bigger agenda they are trying to protect.

Of course proponents usually claim that Heritage Areas are just honorary designations that are designed to enhance tourism. But the bills that they actually write and support have very little to do with driving tourism to the region. Tourism is typically a result of good advertising. The bills have very little to do with advertising, but they have a lot to do with giving these groups power to influence land-use decisions.

When property owners express concern that their property could be taken in the process the proponents always have a ready-made answer. Don't worry, they say, as they quickly point to language in the Heritage Area bills that assure property rights protections. Former Congressman Wolfe actually wrote property rights language into the Heritage Area legislation saying "Nothing in this subtitle…abridges the right of any property owner… including the right to refrain from participating in any plan, project, program, or activity conducted within the National Heritage Area…"

In other words, that language is written to give assurance that that you actually have the right to opt out of the Heritage Area – so, of course, there is absolutely no threat to your property rights. However, further study has shown that this language is basically worthless.

The fact is, it is physically impossible to opt out of an official government boundary when you live inside it. It is also impossible to simply declare that you are going to opt out of any of the land-use regulations, down-zoning, or other restrictions that result from the Heritage Area designation. When your local government passes legislation that affects your property rights because of a Heritage Area, you can't go to them and say, wait a minute. I opt out. They will just laugh.

You don't believe that to be true? Then go down to the County Supervisor's meeting next week and tell them you want to opt out of any rules that say you have to have a building permit for a new porch. See how that works for you!

It must be understood that the Heritage Area affects all the land in the designated area, not just recognized historic sights. The federal designation, made from congressional legislation creating federal regulations and oversight through the National Park Service, requires a contract between state and local governmental entities and the Secretary of the Interior. That contract is to manage the land-use of the region for preservation. That means federal control and zoning, either directly, under the terms of the "management pact", or indirectly. Either way the federal government controls the land-use.

Such "indirect" control is the real danger. In spite of the specific language in the bill which states property rights will be protected, the true damage to homeowners may well come from the private groups, non-governmental organizations (NGOs) and preservation agencies which receive public funds through the Park Service to implement the polices of the Heritage Area.

The funds flowing from the Park Service provide a seductive pork-barrel system for NGO advocacy groups to enforce their vision of development of the Heritage Area. The experience with more than twenty-four such Heritage Areas now in existence nationwide clearly shows such groups will convert this money into political activism to encourage local community and county governments to pass and enforce strict zoning laws. While the tactic makes it appear that home rule is fully in force, removing blame from the federal designation, the impact is fully the fault of the Heritage Areas designation. The result is that private property owners' rights are diminished and much of the local land-use brought to a standstill.

Zoning and land-use policies are and should be local decisions to be made by locally elected officials who are directly accountable to the citizens they represent. However, National Heritage Areas corrupt this inherently local procedure by adding federal dollars, federal oversight, and federal mandates to the mix.

Specifically, when an area is designated a National Heritage Area, the Park Service partners with environmental or historic preservation special interest groups to "restore, preserve, and manage" anything and everything that is naturally, culturally, historically, and recreationally significant to the Heritage Area. This sweeping mandate ensures that every square inch of land, whether private or public is a prime target for regulation or acquisition.

But what of the promised tourism that is supposed to help local communities? Many members of Congress admit they support the concept of

Heritage Areas for that very reason: jobs created by people visiting their little part of the world to see why it's so special. Is it true?

As I have already stated, those boundaries have consequences – strict control over the use of the land. Certain industries may prove to be too "dirty" to satisfy environmental special interests. Eventually such existing industrial operations will find themselves regulated or taxed to a point of forcing them to leave or go out of business. Property that is locked away for preservation is no longer productive and no longer provides the community with tax dollars. Roads most assuredly will be closed (to protect the integrity of the historic area). That means land is locked away from private development, diminishing growth for the community. It also means hunting and recreational use of the land will most certainly be curtailed.

Eventually, such restrictions will take away the community's economic base. Communities with sagging economies become run-down and uninviting. Preservation zoning and lack of jobs force ordinary people to move away. Experience has shown tourism rarely materializes as promised. And it's never enough to save an area economically.

These are the reasons why the specific language in the Heritage Area legislation designed to protect private property rights is basically meaningless to the actual outcome. While the land is not specifically locked away in the name of the federal designation, its very existence creates the pressure on local government to act. The result is the same.

The fact is the Heritage Area designations are completely unnecessary. Most of the historic sites are already under the control of the National Park Service, including Thomas Jefferson's home, Manassas Battlefield (Bull Run – to you Yankees) and Gettysburg Battlefield. Several other birthplaces and significant historic sights are also well preserved.

The boundaries of Gettysburg, for example, were specifically laid out by the men who fought there. Most of the land was private and was donated to the park by the owners more than 125 years ago. While protecting private property and the farms across which the battle raged, they preserved the most significant parts into what today is today a comprehensive memorial.

This old system of voluntary contributions and non-coerced purchases of the land is far superior to a process that uses the massive power of the federal government to rip out the roots of property owners who are simply unlucky enough to live near something that should be special and precious. Given their way, many preservationist special interest groups would set out to turn the entire nation into a museum.

In contrast, it is significant to note that today, as a coercive preservation policy is imposed in Gettysburg, the community has seen the near destruction of its once vital downtown where private businesses are being forced out. Many parts of downtown now are void of significant businesses like clothing shops or hardware stores. Most businesses in the downtown area today are restaurants and tee-shirt shops designed for the tourist industry. That's not the way for a town to build a solid economic future.

Every step of land had something from the past occur on it. But let us remember, those who fought on these fields of "hallowed ground" did so to protect our liberty, including ownership of private property. One must ask how they would react to huge government restrictions over the land now, simply because they fought there. One can envision them again taking up arms to free it from government clutches.

It's interesting to note that the recent protests demanding to remove historic statues have not been opposed by a single Heritage Area management entity. So much for actually defending our American Heritage.

The forces of Sustainable Development have no intention of honoring true American heritage. The rational for preservation legislation is simply another excuse to hide the real goal – reorganizing human society for complete control. The American heritage of individual liberty, free enterprise, and private property isn't even in the equation.

CHAPTER SEVENTEEN

HOW THE UNITED NATIONS TARGETED YOUR MAYOR
IN THE CITIES

San Francisco is the birthplace of the United Nations. On June, 5th, 2005, it was also the location for a major effort by the UN to circumvent national and state governments in order to reorganize human society. Coincidentally, the date was also World Environment Day. This time the UN was targeting mayors from all over the world to enlist them to be soldiers in the Sustainable war.

Like a scene from Michael Crichton's landmark novel *State of Fear*, all of the usual suspects, our self-appointed saviors, were there. There were UN bureaucrats seeking to increase their power and influence, NGOs with their private agendas, Hollywood celebrities acting like authorities on how Americans should rightly live, leaders of corporations seeking to help devise global regulations to kill their competition, and representatives from national and local news outlets that long ago had lost any pretense of delivering unbiased news.

They were all there. UN Secretary General Kofi Annan, along with the host committee, including San Francisco Mayor Willie Brown and Senator Diane Feinstein. Helping to host were the federal Environmental Protection Agency (EPA), and Jonathan Lash of the World Resources Institute. Walking among the crowd were actors Robert Redford and Martin Sheen. As everyone fawned over them, singer Judy Collins could be heard inspiring the gathering with her emotional lyrics. Of course to be expected were representatives from ICLEI. They had recently teamed with Robert Redford and the Mayor of Salt Lake City, Utah to form an environmental congress called the Sundance Summit. Also in attendance were the leaders of the Natural Resources Defense Council (NRDC), the anti-human, rent-a-riot, scaremonger NGO that has worked so diligently to frighten Americans about everything in our society -- from the food we eat, to the chemicals we use and the water we drink. Corporate sponsors included Federal Express, Toyota Prius and Mitsubishi International Corporation Foundation, all dedicated to capitalizing on Sustainable Development practices. They were all ready to do their dance and perform their magic tricks to influence your mayor to join their game.

As the cheerleading and drum circles faded, the gathering got down to the serious business. As part of their participation in the conference, the mayors were pressed to commit their communities to specific legislative and policy goals by signing a slate of United Nations accords. Two documents were presented for the mayors' signatures.

The first document was called the "Green Cities Declaration," a statement of principles which set the agenda for the mayors' assigned tasks. It said, in part, "*Believing as Mayors of cities around the globe, we have a unique opportunity to provide leadership to develop truly sustainable urban centers based on culturally and economically appropriate local actions.*" The Declaration was amazingly bold in that it detailed exactly how the UN intends to implement a very specific agenda in every town and city in the nation. The document included lots of rhetoric about the need to curtail greenhouse gases and preserve resources. But the final line of the Green Cities Declaration was the point of the whole affair: "*Signatory cities shall work to implement the following Urban Environment Accords. Each year cities shall pick three actions to adopt as policies or laws.*"

The raw meat of the agenda was outlined in detail in the second document, called the "Urban Environment Accords." The Accords included exactly 21 specific actions (as in Agenda 21) for the mayors to take, controlled by a timetable for implementation.

Here's a quick look at a few of the 21 agenda actions called for. Under the topic of energy, action item number one called for mayors to implement a policy to increase the use of "renewable" energy by 10% within seven years. Renewable energy includes solar and wind power.

Not stated in the UN documents is the fact that in order to meet the goal, a community would have to reserve thousands of acres of land to set up expensive solar panels and even more land for wind turbines. Consider that it takes a current 50 megawatt gas-fired generating plant about two to five acres of land to produce its power, yet to create that same amount of power through the use of solar panels would require at least 1,000 acres. Using windmills to generate 50 megawatts would require over 4,000 acres of land, while creating a deafening roar and chopping up birds. The cost of such "alternative" energy to the community would be vastly prohibitive, yet such unworkable ideas became the environmentally-correct order of the day that the mayors were being urged to follow.

Perhaps the most egregious action offered in the Urban Environmental Accords dealt with the topic of water. Action item number twenty called for adoption and implementation of a policy to reduce individual water consumption by 10% by 2020. Interestingly, the document begins by stating: "*Cities with potable water consumption greater than 100 liters per capita per day will adopt and implement policies to reduce consumption by 10 percent by 2015.*"

There is no basis for the 100 liter figure other than employing a very clever use of numbers to lower the bar and control the debate. One must be aware that 100 liters equals about 26 gallons per person, per day. According to the UN, each person should only have 10% less than 26 gallons each day to drink, bathe, flush toilets, wash clothes, water lawns, wash dishes, cook, and more.

However, according to the U.S. Geological Survey, Americans need about 100 GALLONS per day to perform these basic functions. Consider also that there is no specific water shortage in the United States. According to the U.S. Environmental Protection Agency, annual water withdrawal across the nation is about 407 billion gallons, while consumption (including evaporation and plant use, is about 94 billion gallons. Such restrictions, as outlined in the Urban Environment Accords, are really nothing more than a dishonest campaign by the UN to control water consumption. That's why in San Francisco the nation's mayors were being pushed to impose policies to take away our free use of water. Control the water, control the people.

The rest of the Accords dealt with a variety of subjects including waste reduction, recycling, transportation, health, and nature. Perhaps the most outrageous promise of action was Action number sixteen in which the mayors were supposed to agree to: "*Every year identify three products, chemicals, or compounds that are used within your city that represents the greatest risk to human health and adopt a law to eliminate their sale and use in the city.*"

There you have it. Every year, our nation's mayors are to promise to ban something! What if there isn't a "chemical or compound" that poses a risk? Gotta ban something anyway!

That's not an idle threat. In the 1990s Anchorage, Alaska had some of the most pristine water in the nation. It had no pollution. Yet the federal government ordered the city to meet strict federal clean water standards that required it to remove a certain percentage of pollution from its water. It's pretty hard to comply with such regulations when the situation simply doesn't exist. But government never was built around logic. Regulations must be obeyed. In order to meet those requirements, Anchorage was forced to dump fish parts into its pristine water so that it could then clean out the required quotas of "pollution." Your city's mayor may have to ban the ink in your fountain pen to meet his quota -- and ban it he will!

What was to be each mayor's reward for destroying private property rights, increasing energy costs on less consumption, and banning something useful every year? He would get green stars! That's right. According to UN documents, if your mayor could successfully complete 8 to 11 of the prescribed 21 actions, the town would get a green star and the designation, "Local Sustainable City." Twelve to 17 actions completed would garner two green stars and the designation, "National Sustainable City." Fifteen to 18 actions completed would bring in three green stars and the title, "Regional Sustainable City." Finally, the energizer bunny mayor who completed 19 to 21 actions completed would get a full four green stars and the ultimate designation of, "Global Sustainable City." Certainly he or she would also get a plaque and get to sit at the head table at the next UN Sustainable Development conference.

Sustainable Development is truly stunning in its all encompassing reach to transform the world into feudal-like governance by making nature the central organizing principle for our economy and society. It is a scheme fueled by unsound science and discredited economics that can only lead modern society down the road to a new Dark Ages of human misery. It is a policy of banning goods and regulating and controlling human action. It is systematically implemented through the creation of non-elected visioning boards and planning commissions. There is no place in the Sustainable world for individual thought, private property or free enterprise. It is the exact opposite of the free society envisioned by this nation's founders.

America's mayors are the elected representatives closest to the people. They are the ones that our founders intended to have the most influence over our daily lives. If the UN succeeds in its efforts to enforce Sustainable Development policy through our mayors, the process will accelerate at an astounding rate and the willingly duped mayors will shockingly realize too late that locally-controlled government will cease to exist. But signs, adorned with green stars, will certainly greet us at every city limit line as the inhabitants, stripped of their property rights, buried under huge tax burdens, and struggling under reduced energy flow, shuffle on as their proud mayor gleams in the global limelight under the banner "think globally and act locally."

Again, the UN's meeting with the mayors took place in 2005. How have local governments responded? Following are a series of reports on the enforcement of Sustainable Development in cities across the nation.

CHAPTER EIGHTEEN

SMART GROWTH AND THE REORGANIZATION OF THE CITIES
IN THE CITIES

Perhaps the largest and farthest-reaching plan for the Sustainable transformation of human society is Smart Growth. We're told Smart Growth policy is necessary to create the community of the future, to guarantee effective planning, and, most importantly, to protect the environment by reducing our carbon footprint to combat climate change.

Most people, when observing the use of the word SMART in reference to community planning or as an attached label to power meters and home appliances, believe it refers to "intelligent," "unique," or "scientific" new ideas for protecting the environment and cutting our carbon footprint. In fact, use of the word SMART is actually engineering lingo meaning:

S - Specific
M - Measurable
A – Achievable
R – Relevant
T – Time Oriented

In other words, use of the acronym SMART means a controlled outcome in a specific period of time.

Should you attend a local public meeting where the community's new "visioning" plan is being promoted, you will be assured that everything has been prepared by your local leaders simply to address unique problems of the community. However, a little research will show, ironically, that almost every community in every state has a nearly identical plan in process, usually ending with numbers like 2030 or 2050. One can also search the internet and find such plans as Jamaica 2050 and Dubai 2050. They cover the world and most importantly - they are all the same basic plan no matter where they are, nationally or globally. One thing they all have in common – none of them are LOCAL!

That's by design because they are all created for the same goal – reorganizing human society in the Sustainable model. Across the United States, most of these plans are being implemented by the same associated planners, fueled by the same grant programs, and aided by the same NGO private groups. Working in well-oiled teams, they cover the nation, reaching out to local and state officials to promote the programs. Each of these NGO groups has their own specific programs to promote, such as bike trails, Heritage Areas, conservation easements, or energy conservation and they bring the grant programs with them for the local officials to apply. It's mostly done in back rooms, out of site of the general public. Unseen hands dig in to decide the community's future.

The sales pitch is for a perfect lifestyle in what they call healthy, happy communities -- where neighbors interact, parents play with their children, and there is no stress from long commutes because all the conveniences of living are just a walk down the street. It all sounds so warm and wonderful, creating images of a near Eighteenth-century atmosphere of peace and tranquility, yet with all the conveniences and technology of our modern age, all leading toward a "sensible growth plan" for future development.

Smart growth planners promote their schemes by insisting that Americans live the wrong way. And they use their comprehensive land-use regulations to impose on others what they insist is the right way to live.

In Omaha, Nebraska, government and NGO forces have been working hard to sell the community on a grand plan for the future called Heartland 2050. Of course, as usual, it's not just for Omaha – but for eight full counties in the surrounding area, all combined into the same regional plan run by an unelected regional council. And the plan openly says it is for the implementation of Sustainable Development.

Listen to the sales pitch. According to the promoters, the goal of Heartland 2050 is to create a strategic "vision" for the region's development over the next 30 years to assure "proper growth." "The Metro area is always changing," say proponents, "but is it moving in the right direction?"

Stop right there! You must ask – moving in the right direction, according to whom? This massive plan will lay the ground rules for transportation, housing, jobs, property/land-use, education, and even health care.

Here's how Smart Growth works. First the planners draw an imaginary line around the community and declare little or no growth will take place outside that line. According to the creed of the planners, growth must be tightly controlled otherwise urban sprawl takes place. It must be stopped.

Why? What is urban sprawl? It is growth outside the pre-determined metro area. It's the building of housing developments that require infrastructure like roads and utilities. Then, of course, such growth causes the creation of shopping malls to serve the needs of the new developments. That, of course, leads to "traffic!" All of those actions are deemed unsustainable by those who appointed themselves our protectors.

The Sustainablists argue that urban sprawl is an added expense to local government, requiring tax dollars to be spent on infrastructure and roads. The answer, they say, is to keep everyone inside the pre-determined line where development, transportation and energy use can be tightly control – all for the common good.

Of course, all of those arguments come with massive holes in them. The new housing developments are built for several reasons. First there is population growth. New families want to start their own homes with all of the advantages, including a place for the kids to play, the personal wealth such an investment provides, and the peace and security a private home of their own brings. Many of these families are escaping the cities because of crime, high taxes and over-crowding. If one could place a video camera at the front door of these new houses to record the home-owning families as they enter for the first time, you would see joy, smiles, and excitement. That's what these new homes mean to the new owners. It used to be called the American Dream. Now such ideas are derided as "sprawl!"

Second, those developments are not a burden on the taxpayers to pay for the infrastructure. Each of those new homes provide increased income for the community through new property taxes. Also, the builders provide the basic streets in the new neighborhoods, In recent years some builders have started to help widen main roads leading to the new developments, in fact that is usually now one of the stipulations for the permit. So the higher taxes argument simply has little basis in fact.

Third, the new shopping malls which spring up around such developments not only provide goods and services for them, they also provide jobs for the new residents. That also adds to the tax rolls. In short, this is how economies are built.

The main enemy of the dedicated Sustainablists is the automobile. To them urban sprawl is the breeder of cars. The sustainable planners have to devise ways to get people out of their cars. That's the first role of Smart Growth.

That means the focus for future housing will be the establishment of high density neighborhoods with residents living in high-rise condos. Walkable communities, as the Sustainablists call them, means the use of private cars will be discouraged in favor of public transportation, bicycles or walking.

How is that done? Several ways. Higher taxes on cars and on gasoline – and there are now plans being developed in various states to tax every mile you drive. Your mileage is kept in the computers of today's cars, like the black boxes in airplanes. Mandatory auto inspections by the state will provide the opportunity to read that information, determine the number of miles driven and a bill will be sent to the car owner each year. Oregon is the first state to announce its intention to collect such taxes, now California has jumped on board.

Heartland 2050 includes the program called the "Complete Street." That is an edict that cars must share the road with bicycles. It calls for "Traffic Calming," which means large speed bumps placed in the center of residential streets that make driving a very unpleasant experience. In addition there are traffic circles that are a menaces to emergency equipment as well as the normal driver. Across the nation, through smart growth plans, communities are now building residential apartment buildings without parking. It's all designed to discourage interest in driving so that residents use bikes for short trips or public transportation, including light rail trains.

In many cities, such as San Francisco, as they eliminate parking from residential areas, they have closed some major streets to vehicle traffic, and have reduced some four-lane streets to two lanes to provide a whole lane for bicycles.

New York City implemented what is called "progressive street projects." They built more than 400 miles of new bike lanes, and they created a massive pedestrian plaza in Times Square by closing five blocks of Broadway to cars.

The announced purpose was to "change the culture." The pedestrian plazas are placed in the center of what were once busy streets, blocking off traffic, and, again, making it difficult to drive in the city. But here, promises the planners, people can congregate, sit at tables in an out of doors atmosphere, and enjoy each other, rather than rushing around by themselves in cars.

One of the leaders of this project said, "*What we're trying to do is see equity of public space. When you build your streets for cars, you're actually building in the expectation that people are going to have cars.*" So, if you stop having streets, obviously people will stop wanting cars.

She went on to explain, "It costs $10,000 per year for a household to own and maintain a car. We're talking about building an affordable option for people to get around." This edict for the drivers of New York City is nothing short of social justice/ social engineering. It's all designed to reduce your ability to drive so that you are forced to use bikes for short trips and public transportation including light rail trains for trips outside the neighborhood. If you want to take a vacation, or visit grandma on Thanksgiving, take the bus, on their timetable and space availability. Of course, forget about taking the kids to see the many Heritage Areas along the way, these buses are not tour buses.

CHAPTER NINETEEN

SELLING THE DREAM!
VIRGINIA BEACH
IN THE CITIES

Virginia Beach, Virginia has produced its "Virginia Beach 2040 plan. Most of the visioning plans for communities around the nation are written in vague language that never quite openly reveals their true purpose. However, the Virginia Beach Vision Plan is one of the most blatantly open and forthright descriptions of the real purpose of Smart Growth ever produced. There is simply no doubt about the planners' goals for the reorganization of Virginia Beach by the year 2040.

The cover of the document carries a graphic that features the words "Diversity," "International," "World-class," "Regional," "Transportation," "Life-Long," and "Learning." That's just a hint of what's to come in this "thoughtful vision for Virginia Beach -- to be achieved by 2040."

First, the document clearly defines what they mean by visioning: "a process of determining a preferred future that draws on the values of the community and hopes for the future. It provides a shared image of life 15-25 year forward. It comes from the future and informs and energizes the present." Apparently time travel has been achieved by the City Fathers in Virginia Beach as a savior has traveled forward and returned with great vision and wisdom to guide the planners.

Next, the Vision 2040 Report uses a series of vignettes of future residents and how they will live as a means to describe the "vision" they have in mind for the community. What will life be like in Virginia Beach in 2040 after the plan is fully in place? Here are direct quotes from the report as the planning committee sets it all down.

QUALITY OF LIFE IN 2040

Our neighborhoods provide a variety of affordable housing alternatives that meet the needs of all people... All people have access too affordable high quality health care and life-long learning opportunities. We are environmentally conscious and a "green" healthy and safe community.... We have a culture of volunteerism and civic engagement.... We support initiatives that strengthen our region.

Yes, sure! Government will decide everyone's needs and desires. The community's future is to be built on government subsidized housing, government subsidized healthcare, life-long indoctrination facilities, all based on top-down control through "sustainable" dictates. And just to make sure all citizens are involved in our well-ordered society we'll order "mandatory volunteerism!"

A CONNECTED COMMUNITY

Virginia Beach is a well-planned community of exciting, diverse neighborhoods, each offering unique opportunities to live, work, play, and grow in a culturally rich and safe environment. Our neighborhoods and residents find interconnectivity through our award winning multi-modal transportation system, the ubiquitous presence of broadband communication technologies, and most importantly by building a deep sense of community.

"Exciting and diverse neighborhoods?" Exactly how is that diversity achieved when all of the neighborhoods are tightly controlled in their buildings, food choices, and education processes, all dictated by a one-size fits all government plan? And don't try to escape. The only way out is on the government-controlled public transportation system. Do prisoners in their cellblocks share a "deep sense of community?"

CONNECTED COMMUNITY — A DAY IN THE LIFE OF GEORGE

George King gets up early to jog before starting his workday. Leaving his condo, he ... meets his jogging partner, Judy. As they continue their run they laugh about the "old days in 2012" when they would have to jump into their cars and meet at a park or gym if they wanted to run together....

After the run...*Since he's running a little late he takes advantage of the car-share system. He steps into the car, gives his code and the car scans the city grid for the most efficient trip to his condo.*

First, we've gotta ask… just how far did they run that he has to get in a car to get home? Second, what if a government-control glitch blocks his code in the electric government provided car? Can he still get home? I'll take those old days in 2012 when my life was still controlled by me!

LEARNING COMMUNITY

We have a comprehensive approach to formal education and broader learning opportunities for citizens of all stages of life that supports their ability to learn, grow, and prosper. We believe in and support an educational continuum that begins at birth and lasts a lifetime. Individuals, families, government and businesses know and accept their roles preparing citizens to be successful throughout their life.

Did you catch that?" Indoctrination begins a birth and everyone "knows and accept their roles…!"

All students entering kindergarten are ready to succeed academically in K-12 because of prenatal care and early childhood initiatives. Students are prepared for success at every stage of their education journey. Teachers are valued and well compensated. There is a zero tolerance for continuous and uncorrected underperforming educators in the classroom.

Teachers are "well compensated?" Was this part written by the National Education Association teachers' union? Do you see one ounce of acceptance of individual choice, wants, or needs in this statement? Prepared in prenatal care? Are children in 2040 created in petri dishes with no parents? Are they simply tools of the state? What happened to kids being kids? Are they allowed to play and have fantasies or is every second of their day taken up in preparation for "success?"

DIVERSE COMMUNITY

City policies, procedures, and results reflect a zero tolerance approach to actions or efforts that stereotype, profile or denigrate any particular segment of the community. The city has negligible gaps in earning potential, unemployment, and overall economic vitality.

There's that phrase "Zero Tolerance" again. You will comply. You will perform to community standards! This also advocates a growing concept in our society – everyone will earn exactly the same amount. So there will be no incentive to be creative or industrious. History has proven that such lack of incentive leads to the collapse of the economy with massive unemployment, and the accompanying lack of goods and services.

THRIVING ECONOMY...IN 2040

Business, academic institutions and governments collaborate to develop and align the skills of the workforce to meet business needs. Businesses are innovative and create partnerships and entrepreneurial opportunities that sustain the economy.

The process for developing the skills of the workforce began in the 1990s under the creation of the Federal Department of Education in programs called Goals 2000, School to Work and Workforce Development Boards. Corporations were assigned the task of deciding what jobs would exist and what kind of workers would be needed in the future, then student curricula were chosen to meet those needs.

Imagine if such boards had been in place in the 1890s. Back then, man moved at the same basic speed as did Alexander the Great a thousand years before – by horseback. And homes were lit the same way – by candlelight. So, the business representatives on such "workforce development boards" of the 1890s would have had long histories of knowing what kind of workers would be needed in the future. They would need farmers, candlestick makers, and buggy whip manufactures. However, they didn't see the coming of some completely unexpected events. Thomas Edison created a system of electricity to light homes, and provide then unheard of electrically powered appliances, cleaning tools and labor saving devices that changed the course of human history. Then Henry Ford changed the age-old transportation system. And the Wright Brothers dared to show man could fly.

That was all individual innovation that no government bureaucrat could ever foresee or direct. It's the very reason why Socialism, which controls and stifles man's motivation and creativity, fails. It is obvious that Sustainable Development is designed to assure that never again will society allow another Thomas Edison, Henry Ford or Wright brothers to disrupt their well-ordered society. They should be hung as heretics.

Wind and alternative energy industries help drive the economy. No they don't and they won't. They don't work. European cities that have tried to use alternative energy have seen their economies collapse and are now desperately returning to fossil fuels to provide energy needs. Maybe a better alternative to fossil fuels will be developed by 2040, but not if individual creativity is destroyed by government straight-jackets.

BOLD STEPS: REGIONALISM

City Council leads the effort to build a strong, effective regional coalition to leverage the region's assets and creates a culture of collaboration for the success of the Southern Chesapeake Bay Region. We can only succeed as a region. Everyone in the region wins. Region speaks with one political voice/clout.

Regionalism is being used to destroy locally-elected representative government. Regionalism is the fantasy playground of the NGOs who gain power without the consent of the people. And, of course, that is the goal. Later in this book I will provide a complete discussion on Regionalism and why it is a threat.

STRATEGIC GROWTH AREAS (SGA)
AREAS DESIGNATED TO ABSORB FUTURE GROWTH IN OUR CITY

Rather than relying on the dwindling inventory of remaining undeveloped land/ the SGAs will accommodate growth at higher densities, thereby averting continued suburban sprawl. Each SGA has a long-range masterplan which describes the future vision and guides policy decisions for growth and development in each area.

SGAs are used by the planners to control growth and direct where development is allowed to take place. The tight controls on land eventually severely limit availability, driving up housing costs. This is done by enforcing regulations on what kinds of development is allowed. Is it residential or preserved for agriculture? How is that controlled? By limiting powerlines, cable access, cell towers, and the like which will only be allowed in the designated growth areas. Woe to the homeowner who finds himself living in the non-growth areas without these services. And woe to the homeowner who wants to build a home on land designated to be agriculture. Freedom of choice and property ownership? Not with the common good at stake!

This is Smart Growth. This is where Sustainable Development policies are leading the nation's local communities. Again, each of the examples in italics were taken directly from the Virginia Beach 2040 Committee Report. This is truly what they intend for the community. Worse, it is the real goal behind the planning projects for every city in the nation, whether they display it this openly or not. As you read the Virginia Beach plans do you see any reference to Free Enterprise, Individualism or Private Property? Is this what you hope your future will be? What kind of life does this leave for your children and grandchildren? Every parent must look forward and ask these questions.

CHAPTER TWENTY

TOOLS FOR THE TRANSFORMATION
IN THE CITIES

Smart Growth is being imposed on our cities in order to transform them into government-controlled spheres. The programs being used to achieve this dominion come in many names and in many forms. Each one is just a small piece to the whole puzzle. Perhaps as a single program each could be harmless, maybe a few are good ideas. However, fused together they become a threat that destroys private property, controls living habits and divides populations into specific categories making each more easily directed.

Programs like Historic Preservation of downtown neighborhoods, implementation of bike lanes in "share the road" programs, public transportation programs, affordable housing projects, and environmental protection projects all have their specific advocates. A look into the workings at City Hall will reveal multiple NGO groups and planners all working in lockstep behind closed doors, huddled with elected officials and planning departments to form a well-organized matrix that eventually morphs into the community long-rang visioning plan.

As a result, there is a near endless number of programs and processes being used in cities across the nation to impose the plan. Most are funded by federal grants, especially through HUD, EPA and the Department of Transportation. Again, all have their own NGO or planning group doing the heavy lifting to promote them and assure that communities take the grants to put them in place. Of course, as spotlights are put on these programs and citizens begin to understand their threat, the cleaver NGOs and federal agencies quickly change their names – but not their purpose. Meanwhile more programs are constantly invented, all with the same goal – Sustainable Development. However, here are just a few current programs to watch for as your community drives forward with new development projects.

FORM-BASED CODE

Form-based code "is a means of regulating land development to achieve a specific urban form," according to their own literature. Form-based code is a plan for regulating the form, scale and character of buildings. It coordinates floor area ratios, dwelling units per acre (Smart Growth pack-em and stack-em condos), parking ratios, and more. It assures all buildings are consistent and predictable as they are the same size and design, with the same set-backs, plantings and functions; in short, it prevents any distinctions in buildings. So basically, all communities will eventually look exactly alike. As it says in its own literature, Form-based codes are regulatory, not advisory, and therefore enforceable, based on the International Building Codes (IBC) that are being enforced in cities across the nation and the world. In reality, Form-based codes are the fulfillment of the description of the "ideal communist city," as discussed earlier in the section "What is Sustainable Development."

HUMAN RIGHTS CITIES

Human Rights Cities are municipalities "that refers explicitly to the (United Nations) Universal Declaration of Human Rights and other international human rights standards…" In short, social justice principles override the rule of law. They are sold as a means to properly address "urban problems" such as traffic congestion, insufficient public services, racial discrimination, economic human rights, the rights of children, and of course, affordable housing. Essentially, Human Rights Cities translates to mean United Nations cities. Human Rights Cities are the embodiment of the entire UN Sustainable Development agenda of top-down control over every human thought and action.

WHAT WORKS CITIES

What Works Cities are located in every region of the United States and in 37 states. This NGO operation supplies communities with workshops, training, data, and all the information and evidence needed to guide your city into the "right" programs that work. It is viewed as a useful tool by local governments to assure they are doing it right. By adopting the WWC Standard, the community becomes part of a national network of local governments. In short, they will be fully invaded by armies of NGOs to help them "do it right!" Of course, all What Works Cities policy is based on Sustainable Development programs.

TRANSITION

Transition: If the goal is to reorganize human society, why not organize a challenge to the inmates so they can come up with new ideas on how it's to be done. Says the literature, "The aim of "Transition" is to help you be the catalyst in your community for an historic push to make where you live more resilient, healthier, and bursting with strong local livelihoods, while also reducing its ecological footprint." So let's all sit around our living room tonight and think up ways to make government bigger and more intrusive in everyone else's lives. So we now have Transition "towns, cities, neighborhoods, projects, enterprises, universities, schools, livelihoods." And now you know why we have high school and college kids attacking anyone who disagrees with their positions on the dire threat of global warming, the racism of private property ownership and fascistic free enterprise. Let's form a Transition group to boycott the restaurant that serves meat, let's block the roads so cars can't pass, and let's march in protest through Walmart to denounce profits and capitalism. For we are in Transition!

PROMISE ZONES

Promise Zones "are partnerships between the federal government and local agencies aimed at creating jobs, leveraging private investment, increasing economic activity, expanding educational opportunities, and reducing violent crime." Amazing. It used to be so clear. Private enterprise created jobs and therefore prosperity, which lead to private investment, which increased economic activity. And government's job was to arrest violent criminals. We even gave government the job of running the education system. Government failed miserably at its basic tasks, so now criminals pretty much control the neighborhoods and no one is learning anything in schools. Then government started to involved itself into the "proper" ways business should be run, so now we have a lack of jobs and, therefore, economic activity and investment. So, how do we fix the crisis that is the result? We come up with partnerships between private interests groups and government to do more of the same bad government. Only this time government can have an excuse as to why there is a crisis – we were all in partnership. And as we pursue this folly let's completely delude ourselves about what we are doing and call it a "promise zone." How about calling it a "Wing and a Prayer." It will produce the same results. Don't forget, all of the private organizations joining in this partnership to promote their own private agendas get to feed off the grant money too. Private enterprise would have done it all on its own dime while taking all the risks and would have achieve what they intended without the bribery.

CHAPTER TWENTY-ONE

SUSTAINABLE DEVELOPMENT
SMART GROWTH FAILS
IN THE CITIES

So, how will all of this afect us? Will life in the community improve as promised by the planners? For the best evidence available to predict the future one must simply look at where all of this has already been tried. Over a decade ago, Portland, Oregon, was announced as the poster child for Smart Growth policy. There it was nearly fully implemented.

You can take an airplane over Portland and actually see the Smart Growth line around the city. On one side is vast, dense development. On the other side is nothing but open land, locked away from human use.

Today, local planners assure the community that they want citizen input – that each will have a say in every aspect of the plan. Yet, surveys show that over 85% of Americans want to live in single-family homes with yards and driveways. But smart growth planners ignore that fact.

Instead, the plans call for major controls on suburban housing development out of concern for future population growth. Housing to provide for growing population density becomes the concern.

You see, once the ban on suburban development is in place, there is now a controlled living area. It doesn't grow. What happens when the population of the community does grow? It gets crowded and more densely populated building has to go up, not out.

As reported by Smart Growth opponent, the late Dr. Michael Coffman, those advocating Smart Growth can become so obsessive they become irrational. For instance, on June 18, 2001, the Sierra Club defined "efficient urban density" as a city containing 500 housing units to the acre. Put another way, 500 families would have to live on an acre of land which is 209x209 feet! This would require a 14-story apartment building of 36 very small 1,000 square foot units (with hallways) occupying each floor. Increasing the apartment size to 1500 square feet would require a 21-story building!

After being criticized that such densities were more than thee times greater than the highest density tracts in Manhattan and more than double the most dense and squalid ward of Bombay, India, the Sierra Club quickly revised its definition of urban efficiency to 100 units per acre. Reaching even that goal, however, would require living arrangements that are 2.4 times as dense as all Manhattan, twice as dense as central Paris and ten times that of San Francisco, according to the Heritage Foundation. The density of the average suburban area is 1-3 unites per acre.

True to Sustainable zealotry, in Portland, the planners kept upping the density requirements for housing. To increase urban densities, the planners turned dozens of neighborhoods of single-family homes into apartments and condos. If you owned a vacant lot, you could not build a single-family house on it – you would have to build a rowhouse or apartment. In some cases, the restrictions were so strict that if your house burned down, you could not rebuild a single-family home on the property.

Eventually, Portland planners decided that rowhouses and low-rise apartments were not enough. They changed the rules to enforce the building of high rise apartment buildings. Then they gave tax breaks, below-market land sales, and other subsidies to developers who built the high-rises. That meant that traditional neighborhoods were invaded by high-rise developments.

In Portland, the center of the plan was the light rail train system, a 125 mile transit system. As they planned the rail line, planners began to reduce roadway capacities for cars, promising that the rail line would result in less congestion. The planners gleefully announced that the most desirable homes would be those along the rail line. This would assure convenience for ridership, they claimed. Whoops. Independent studies reveal that the people living in them don't ride public transit any more than residents in single-family neighborhoods. As a result, developers refused to build high-density housing along the transit corridors because there was little market for them. So Portland, and other cities, now have now begun to offer tens of millions of dollars in subsidies (tax dollars) for such developments.

In Atlanta, Georgia, the push was on to build a light rail transportation system. One resident studied the plan, took the official estimated construction cost and overlaid that with the number of predicted riders of the system and found that, with the predicted cost of the system, he could buy every single rider their own limo and even throw in a driver. Across the country plans for light rail train systems rarely, if ever, meet original cost estimates. Most costs skyrocket out of sight. Moreover, thousands of acres of private property is taken for the right of way.

The result of Portland's grand plan is that increased density has destroyed the neighborhood atmosphere. Congestion is worse, housing and consumer costs are higher and urban services such as fire, police, and schools have declined as the city took money from these programs to subsidize the high-density developers.

Now for those worried about social equity and the needs of the poor and minorities, results are showing that Smart Growth policy is a very bad deal for the poor. The economics of Smart Growth are sobering and hit few harder than the poor. As growth boundaries limit space, new home construction drives up housing prices beyond the reach of most.

Studies show that prior to the Smart Growth surge in the 1990s, an average home cost just 2.5 to 3 times the median income of community residents. So a person earning $40,000 annually could likely purchase a home for $120,000.

But in 2006, in Smart Growth cities like Boston, Portland and San Diego, homes respectively cost 6.5 and 10.5 times the median family income. Homes costing just four times more than annual incomes are considered "seriously unaffordable." Today, a family in San Diego earning $125,000 would be hard-pressed to afford a home 10 times that amount. In San Jose, California, Smart Growth polices caused housing prices to nearly double as density increased to more than 5,000 people per square mile.

Again in Portland, the city has just announced a new regulation to force homeowners to have the government conduct Home Energy Surveys to force compliance with Sustainable energy regulations before their homes can be put on the market and listed for sale. Meanwhile, homebuilders are now vastly reducing plans for building new homes because Portland is running out of buildable land, even though outside the tightly controlled urban growth boundary there is plenty. As the population continues to grow, home availability will disappear. High-rise condos will become smaller and smaller until they are little more than dormitories.

For those who believe that Sustainable programs play a major role in helping the poor, think again. A considerable amount of research has shown that automobiles are essential for helping low income families get out of poverty. According to a report from University of California researchers Steven Raphael and Lorien Rice, "...if you have a car you are more likely to have a job and earn money. For that reason, Smart Growth anti-car policies are a direct threat to the poor. In addition, these Smart Growth economic realities are now forcing low-income and young people out of their ethnic neighborhoods and into public housing programs as expensive high-rise condos replace their homes and destroy their local businesses. So much for the promise of diversity. The poor have little hope of ever buying a home and experiencing what used to be called the American dream."

In Portland, after decades of Smart Growth development, exorbitant living costs have driven over 10,000 minority families out of their urban homes. In the San Francisco Bay area, thousands of low-income families are being uprooted from their homes and relocated, often against their will, into "Preferred Development Areas." In Seattle, the city government intends to charge a new construction tax to pay for government housing – raising prices even higher.

Smart Growth, Sustainable Development and all of their grand sounding names are part of a special purpose. Hidden in all of the feel-good rhetoric is a political agenda based on redistribution of wealth and control of resources. That's how to control populations and transform human society to your own political agenda. Agenda 21.

CHAPTER TWENTY-TWO

HOMEOWNERS ASSOCIATIONS
IN THE CITIES

As government storms out of control, citizens try to find ways to reel it back in and avoid being run over by oppressive regulations. Such is the promise of Home Owner Associations (HOA).

The sales pitch is protection of property values, individual participation and a larger voice in the decisions of the community, and "carefree living," with the family safely protected from crime, gangs, and the nut cases that populate so many neighborhoods these days.

The number of Homeowners Associations has grown dramatically since the concept was first introduced fifty years ago. In 1970 there were 10,000 communities under HOA rule, affecting about 2.1 million home-owners. By 2016 the number had skyrocketed to 342,000 communities with 69 million residents, or 21.3% of the nation's population. One could assume from such massive growth that HOAs are highly successful and wildly popular. That would be a mistake.

In fact, rather than protect residents from out-of-control government, HOAs have grown precisely because of state legislatures and local government municipalities mandating the creation of HOAs through local zoning ordinances that ensure their proliferation. It's nearly impossible to buy property in a residential neighborhood today without being forced to join an HOA.

After purchasing the home and force to abide by HOA rules, residents quickly find that their new community has its own built-in set of gangs and nutcases. These are found in the personage of HOA board members or others involved in its management. If that sounds harsh, consider the following examples.

» Many state legislatures across the country have enacted laws allowing HOA board members to adopt rules and regulations, find a homeowner in violation of one of more of these rules then to issue a fine for the violation, and foreclose "non-judicially" (meaning not having to go to court). Then the HOAs can sell the house out from under the owners – all with the support of state law.

» Homeowners, unaware of such laws are at the mercy of power-hungry HOA board members as they are routinely sued, fined, or otherwise punished for such violations as painting their doors a different color, placing a flag in their yard, or putting up Christmas lights or religious symbols. INFRACTION, say the Board. And the homeowner is forced to spend thousands of dollars on legal fees to defend themselves, or possibly find a lien placed on their home.

» There are reported cases of HOAs actually forbidding children to play outside their homes. No neighborhood football games, riding bikes, or just normal playtime outside. Of course, the excuse from the board was concern for "safety." In one such HOA, when parents began to complain and fight back they were threatened with more fines, harassment, the filming and video recordings of their kids.

» HOAs routinely enter onto private property looking for infractions. The use of drones is now being considered to fly over ones property, taking pictures so the Board can levy fines for having an un-approved garden hose in the back yard that no one can see. In some cases, particularly in high-rise condos, HOAs have keys to al properties. The excuse is precaution against leaks from your or neighboring units. That makes sense, of course. But this "privilege" is often abused by vindictive administrators as they will use the keys to "inspect" the interior of the unit. There have been reported cases in which such "inspections" resulted in the moving of personal items in the home – just to drive the homeowner nuts as a form of harassment.

» And finally, unlike the three branches of government, in an HOA there is no separation of powers. The board as a whole, the president acting on his or her own, and the manager, come up with "rules and regulations". There is no oversight as to whether they have the authority to adopt these rules or not. Many times the rules are simply a "knee-jerk" reaction to a pet peeve of one of those in power. Then, that same group in power finds the homeowner in contempt of their rules as they levy fines and punishment. Again, the homeowner is fined and led to foreclosure on the home, not because the owner is in arrears of the HOA dues, but because they were fined for perhaps letting their grass grow an extra quarter of an inch over the allowed height.

» In 2016, HOAs collected $88 billion from homeowners. This money is supposed to provide for services including street maintenance, sidewalks, streetlights, trash and snow removal. However, its important to note that homeowners pay property taxes for those same services. In short, HOA dues are a form of double taxation. Moreover, homeowners are routinely denied access to HOA accounting books and records. Even getting a court order doesn't help.

How can anyone feel safe and secure in their own homes when such actions come armed with powers and heavy fines come sanctioned by state legislatures? While people are sold on the positive concept of an HOA as a means of security and protection, it often turns into a living nightmare where they are forced to fight their neighbors just for the right to live in their own homes.

The power-mongers of the HOAs use their positions to dictate how they want others to behave, according to their own desires. In their drive for control they quickly forget that these are people simply trying to raise their children and live their lives in peace and the safety of their own homes.

Most importantly, HOAs are a major tool in the growing push toward the enforcement of Smart Growth through the establishment of Public/ Private Partnerships. In this way, housing will eventually be funded by government and managed by non-government entities – i.e. Home Owners Associations. It's all part of the drive to reorganize human society for Agenda 21/Sustainable Development.

CHAPTER TWENTY-THREE

REGIONALISM
IN THE CITIES

> "*Regionalism must precede globalism. We foresee a seamless system of governance from local communities, individual states, regional unions and up through the United Nations itself.*"
> - The UN Commission on Global Governance

The American Founders wisely organized our nation so that local government would have the most influence over our daily lives specifically because local citizens would also have the most influence over the local government and its actions. Such a system was designed to bring harmony and balance, leading to the utmost freedom in self-governance.

If your goal is to change human society through top-down control, then your mission must be to change that system. But how do you eliminate local control without causing an uprising? Simple. Make up an entire vocabulary for previously unheard of needs for government intervention and then create emergencies to make it all necessary.

As we saw in the Wildlands Project, the goal has been set to "rewild" 50% of all the land in every state, back to the way it was before human settlements destroyed the natural environment. This requires total control of every inch of the land to determine where "human settlements" may be and which land is to remain unused. Then, it's necessary to get those nasty humans off the rural lands and into the cities. Smart Growth.

What is the vocabulary necessary to set the process in place? If we are going to herd people off their land and convert it to wilderness we need to remap the entire area. We start talking in very intellectual sounding terms about "wilderness areas" where specific species live. And then we need to make room for them to roam unmolested by humans. So we call these "wilderness corridors," inside of which no human activity will be allowed. No cities, no roads, no individual homes or farms.

Of course we can't just lock away this land all at once, there are people living there, after all – homes, and farms, perhaps small villages. So we need a plan to slowly remove them without causing alarm. Thus, in such areas, we will establish "buffer zones." Then we will set specific "conservation objectives" for the buffer zones with the primary objective of "restoration and rehabilitation" to repair and restore "damaged eco-systems." To accomplish all of this will require severe rules and regulations to assure that animals run free and the humans are penned up. Eventually, those humans still living in the buffer zone find it impossible to stay and so they leave, headed for other areas more acceptable to human activity. At that point, the buffer zone becomes part of the expanded wilderness area and a new buffer zone is established as the process begins again.

Eventually, through this process, people are systematically and effectively moved off the land and herded into megacities. We will call those cities "zones of cooperation." The cities are surrounded by "urban growth boundaries" that restrict "sprawl" and assure humans activity is strictly contained within.

Now we must assure that such cities abide by the new rules for human habitat; we can't trust individual cities that are controlled by the election process to assure the proper rules are maintained. That's why the areas are called zones of cooperation as it's vital that we establish a system of cooperation with all of these human settlements in the "region."

We will need an organized system of oversight to open communications and oversee the daily operation of the designated human habitat. Certainly we will have representatives of people living in each of the cities. But we must also have dedicated, environmentally-enlightened representatives of the proper and trusted Non-governmental organizations as well. Each will be appointed to a governing body that shall be called a "regional council."

The regional councils are organized to fulfill a specific agenda to assure that every city complies with this agenda. Elected local governments, and eventually state legislatures, will begin to lose their power and influence in directing policy as the non-elected regional councils take charge over multiple counties and communities in the designated region. They will eventually answer to larger regional councils that oversee multiple states. Such regional councils do not adhere to city, county or state boundaries, instead they follow specifically designated and tightly controlled environmental zones. The Sierra Club has suggested that North America be divided into 21 eco-regions. These regions do not comply with any national boundaries.

Through regionalization of government, elections become irrelevant, private property disappears, and individual wants and needs are ignored. It becomes impossible to discuss problems with elected officials who no longer wield authority. Instead you will now be referred to the proper commission, department, or council to handle your issue. There you will find another appointed hack with his/her own agenda, not caring about your situation. In short, regionalism, combined with Smart Growth, is the demise of local representative government.

Once the regional council is entrenched, citizen input is ignored. Community opposition is of no consequence. In a Providence, Rhode Island planning hearing, the roomful of local residents were outraged at a state led economic development program called Rhode Map Rhode Island. It was a raw social engineering scheme citizens did not want. After heated comments, the unelected board voted unanimously to advance the plan.

Portland, Oregon's regional council used its power over the local communities to ignore local opposition and negative votes simply by rubber-stamping the plans without debate or public input.

These and hundreds of similar events are the untold shame of the establishment of non-elected government through Regional Sustainable Development.

The EPA is a major force in pushing Smart Growth programs. Says the EPA promotional materials, "The layout of a city or county and access to public transportation can hugely affect the carbon footprint and overall sustainability of the region."

Every decision is made based on the pre-determined agenda. As clearly stated by Reed Noss (one of the creators of the Wildlands Project), "The native ecosystems and the collective needs of non-human species must take precedence over the needs and desires of humans." That, then, is the clear plan of regionalism.

This is what the UN's Commission on Global Governance meant by a "seamless system of governance" from your local community to the UN itself. That is what former Soviet leader Mikhail Gorbachev meant when he address the State of the World Forum, saying, the United Nations "inevitably, must assume some aspects of world government."

Smart Growth combined with Regionalism are the two-pronged attack to crush free enterprise, private property and individual rights in a drive for total top-down control. The good news is that such total control is not yet fully in place and some local officials are beginning to see the dangers and at least ask some questions in opposition. It is still possible to stop it if the local citizens understand what is being done and why it is dangerous. Here are 10 Reasons to rise up and say no!

10 REASONS TO AVOID REGIONAL PLANS

This is a report on a Regionalism program in New York State with special thanks for details provided by John Anthony of Sustainable Freedom Lab.

Planning is not a one-size-fits-all exercise. Yet, that is exactly what regional plans attempt, while gradually silencing local officials and the public.

Here are 10 reasons to avoid implementing regional plans and councils. Cleaner Greener NY, also called the Capital Region Sustainability Plan (CRSP), is a model of why community members and local public officials must work together and say "NO" to regionalization and regional planning.

See how many apply to your region's proposal.

1. **Planners gain miniscule community participation when forming the regions, the plans or the councils.**

There are over 1 million residents in the proposed CRSP. Despite claims of "stakeholder engagement", less than 300 participated in planners' workshops. In CRSP surveys, only 96 people, or less than .0001 percent of residents participated.

2. **Plans are prepackaged and do not represent unique community needs.**

In spite of claims to the contrary, most plans encompass the same government sponsored top-down "livability" control features. CRSP includes the same "livable communities", fewer vehicle miles traveled, and increased compact living as most regional plans. Cleaner Greener NY (CGNY) further promises the government and non-governmental organization pushed (NGO) standbys of virtually every plan: confiscation of open spaces, forced environmental justice, hi-speed rails, and dilution of privately controlled farmland interests through conservation easements.

3. Plans do not protect individual property rights.

Few regional plans mention the potential individual property rights infringements, tax increases or loss of potential wealth accumulation inherent in most proposals. None offers any method for protection against such losses. The CRSP contains no enforceable landowner protections.

4. Plans fail to protect communities against onerous regulations passed by regional councils.

Once installed, regional councils or consortiums have immense power to pass regulations with minimal or no local input. The CRSP offers a seat for council representatives. However, having a community representative sitting on a larger multi-county consortium is not the same as making planning decisions with local citizens and local public officials working together in your hometown.

5. Plans rely on questionable "experts" for critical advice.

The CRSP relies on the Apollo Alliance for assurances there will be green jobs, which are fundamental to the plan's success. Yet, Apollo advised on the 'stimulus program' assuring there would be shovel ready and green jobs if passed. A year later, it was learned Apollo exaggerated the job potential.

6. Plans release questionable or incomplete statistics, which create false impressions.

In the case of Cleaner, Greener NY, the plan optimistically depends on green jobs, stating the US had a 9.1% increase in these between 1998 and 2007. The authors omitted that NY actually lost 1.9% of their green jobs during that same period. They also failed to notify community members that Congressional hearings cast serious doubt on the permanency, quality or even existence of the green jobs claimed.

7. Promotes community solutions without explaining the potential negative effects.

The CRSP promotes conservation easements to protect farmland from development without addressing the loss of dominant estate status, potential for plan changes, the downsides of 'best practices' and a host of ways in which landowners can lose their property and its value while still technically being the owner.

8. Councils open the door for government grants, which often contain restrictive policies to reduce vehicle use while forcing low-income housing and social justice.

The CRSP states that future grant monies will be necessary, but there is no details provided as to their source nor of any stipulations that will be attached.

9. Regional councils confiscate much of local officials' power, leaving the community with less representation.

In the CRSP, 25 local officials have already diminished their oversight by agreeing to allow the state government in Albany to take the lead in all grant processing. To protect constituents, public officials must carefully study all grants and report the implications to their constituents before approval. Grants are the doorway to regulatory control of community members' lifestyles, activities and residential opportunities. In NY, communities are already beginning to pay the price for regionalization before the plan is even approved.

10. Once formed, regional councils are virtually irreversible.

Once officials agree to form a region and council, if community members discover they dislike its regulations, how can they disband the entity and roll back the dictates? There is no provision in the CRSP for its break up or regulatory rollback.

REGIONAL GOVERNMENT - WHERE NO ONE CLAIMS TO BE RESPONSIBLE!

Jennie Granato is a tax-paying citizen of Montgomery County, Ohio. She and her family own a 165-year-old historic house and farm just outside of Dayton where they've lived for forty years. On July 31, 2013, Jennie's front yard was demolished – thanks to county and planning commission bureaucrats!

The Miami Valley Regional Planning Commission (MVRPC) began seizing people's private property for its "essential" project – a $5-million bike path extension! Jennie knew something was going to affect her property, but was never told to what extent. Jennie and her family tried for over a year to negotiate and reason with this unelected regional commission. The county and its appraisers kept stalling, saying they wanted a meeting with Jennie, even as they ignored her pleas and offered a pittance for taking her front yard, and thus driving the value of her home down to close to worthless.

The meeting never came – and officials didn't even allow Jennie's uncle to speak at a hearing. But the bulldozers certainly came! One day in 2013, with no warning, they just started demolishing trees and the hedge that protected Jennie's yard from the highway that ran in front of her home. The government seized almost all of Jennie's front lawn. The bike "highway" now comes within five feet of her front door!

Jennie's 84-year-old mother heard the commotion and ran outside to see what it was. She entered the yard just in time to see the bulldozers push over her beloved Magnolia tree, where she had spent many a summer day as she sat in her swing underneath it. In shock, Jennie's mother grabbed her chest as she fell over and died.

Of course the government refused to accept any responsibility for this tragedy. It was just promoting the "public welfare" of the private "stakeholders" and pressure groups it works with. When she complained to her county commissioners she was told it was up to the regional council. The regional council said they had nothing to do with it other than to apply for the grant. **No one was responsible!**

That response has become far too common. The government and these groups grab more and more control over our lives, more power to tell us what we can and cannot do with our property. But they accept no transparency and no accountability. This is a major danger of unelected regional governments. They are not dependent on the citizens at the ballot box and therefore not responsive to your complaints. This is one way government is spiraling out of control.

CHAPTER TWENTY-FOUR

HUD, EPA, DOT, AFFH AND SOCIAL ENGINEERING
IN THE CITIES

The federal department of Housing and Urban Development (HUD) is a major player in the implementation and enforcement of Sustainable Development. Through every administration, from Clinton to Obama, including Republican and Democrat presidents, the policies have been moved forward relentlessly. Today, even as Dr. Ben Carson sits at the top of HUD for the Trump Administration with promises to reign in the agency, at least 90% of the agency's personnel are holdovers from the previous administration. That means little has so far changed.

In 2009, Barack Obama formed the Partnership for Sustainable Communities which resulted in the merging of the power, overreach, and money of HUD, the Department of Transportation (DOT), and the Environmental Protection Agency (EPA). The purpose was to strengthen the power of the federal government to push federal planning initiatives on local communities. Specifically, Obama wanted to force individual communities to adopt the government's "Livability Principles." If they refused they would face loss of grant money from these agencies.

The Livability Principles are the guidelines for communities to destroy existing neighborhoods through Smart Growth, thereby forcing families to live in the dense populations of the stack-em and pack-em high-rise condos. The grants accepted by the communities are the enforcement tool. Take the grant, then prepare a comprehensive plan to match those rules. Further, the Livability Principles also called for the creation of more open-space by ensuring those plans included trading valuable private property for public parks and shared spaces, along with including plans to reduce the use of automobiles.

HUD's 2010 "Sustainable Communities Regional Development Grant Program" specifically ordered communities to meet "mandatory outcomes from the creation of the regional plan for sustainable development." Failure to do so creates a violation of the grant and opens the community to lawsuits for being out of compliance.

The Livability Principles, and the combination of HUD, EPA and DOT working together to enforce them on cities, brought the whole Sustainable plan together, from the Wildlands Project to Smart Growth.

The EPA's Challenge Grant Program from 1998 made that clear saying: "*The formerly rejected 'Wildlands Project,' designed to migrate Americans into controlled regions; and the Vancouver Action Plan's goal to increase government's control over private property, were jointly transformed into America's 'Regional Sustainable Development' movement.*" That one sentence brought together the U.S. federal government with the United Nations Sustainable Development global plan, clearly revealing the intent to move people off the rural lands and into controlled cities, where private property rights were to be tightly controlled or eliminated. And now the federal government had the means to do it through Barack Obama's enforcement of the Livability Principles.

In 2002, HUD provided funds to the American Planning Association to create boilerplate Smart Growth legislation to be enacted by local governments that enabled the federal government's plans. The APA created the Growing Smart Legislative Guidebook to be used by every community to provide direction for creating "local" policy. Among other things, the Guidebook recommends that city councils and county commissions use "takings" legislation to confiscate the property of individuals who failed to change their property to conform to government plans. Using those guidelines, cities across the nation began to draw the Smart Growth boundaries around their borders and declare tightly-controlled "Strategic Growth Areas."

In addition, "Regional Smart Growth Planning" began to take hold through these guidelines. Thrive 2055 is a proposed region that would cover 16 counties in Tennessee, Georgia, and Alabama. The plan would not only do away with local political boundaries and city limits, it would also erase state boundaries as it creates a single region. Local and state elected governments would find severe challenges to their ability to govern as the public elected them to do. Of course, inside such regions private property simply does not exist.

In 2015 the Department of Transportation issued the Smart City Challenge to create a "City of the Future." The Challenge calls for community planners to come up with innovative and sharable ideas that create "opportunities to connect mixed-income housing with transit or economic development initiatives to locate new jobs within a region along highly-accessible multimodal corridors." DOT was excited to promote the program saying, "We encourage cities to develop their own unique vision, partnerships and blueprints to demonstrate to the world what a fully integrated, forward-looking transportation network looks like." To encourage cities to get involved in the challenge, the DOT partnered with a planning group called Vulcan, Inc., offering up to $40 million as a prize for the best plan. Sustainable public transportation that eliminated the use of automobiles and the need for more highways would lead to the winning design.

Meanwhile in the cities, HUD issued its Community Challenge Planning grants using strict guidelines for "inclusionary zoning ordinances" and land acquisition, altering building codes and boosting construction of mixed use and affordable housing.

In 2013, in a speech before the NAACP, HUD Secretary Shaun Donovan clearly revealed HUD's determination to take control of American cities and neighborhoods in the name of fair housing when he said, "There are no stones we won't turn. There are no places we won't go. And there are no complaints we won't explore in order to eliminate housing discrimination."

In 2015, HUD issued a new 377-page ruling called Affirmatively Furthering Fair Housing (AFFH). The purpose is further enforcement of Smart Growth through social justice standards instead of the rule of law. Affordable Housing has become the new battle cry to oppose free enterprise, property rights, and individual wants and needs in favor of the collective. Property ownership is now called "racism" and "white privilege" as "community property" replaces private property through Sustainable Development.

AFFH is the tool of choice for that fight. To achieve its goals, AFFH requires local government agencies that apply for HUD grants to provide a massive profile of the community, including detailed income levels of residents, the breakdown of various religions affiliations and populations, color and national origin of the population, all broken down by neighborhood. Then, using the Livability Principles, HUD determines any "imbalances" in the makeup of the neighborhoods. If necessary, HUD then forces a major shift of the "proper" people into certain neighborhoods to assure the desired "balance." Every five years communities must supply HUD with updates on the progress to achieve balance to assure progress. This is top-down dictatorship by the national government and is nothing less than social engineering!

The next step for communities that fail to comply to AFFH rules is to bring lawsuits. And HUD has begun to file a bunch of them. There is one major problem in dealing with AFFH lawsuits -- there is no set definition as to what AFFH compliance is. Instead it's whatever HUD claims it is. All they need to start legal action is a complaint against the community.

To assure there are plenty of complaints, HUD expects each city to invite participation in their planning programs by civil rights groups, affordable housing developers, community development organizations and any interested members of the public to assist in identifying potential areas of discrimination. Does anyone notice a problem with this situation? The very groups that benefit from these program, NGOs, agitators, and multiple special interests assure that problems will be found and lawsuits will be filed

For example, in Baltimore, Maryland, the NAACP discovered that the community put Section 8 Public Housing in the same areas of the city. This situation, they claimed, caused ghettos as low-income people, combined with drug dealers, MS13 gangs and others, all seemed to congregate together, creating a high crime area. So the NAACP filed a lawsuit. And they won. The result of the suit -- Baltimore must now spend $30 million of local taxpayer money to begin to build 1,000 low-income housing units inside upscale neighborhoods over the next ten years. That, says the NAACP, will make it all fair. Never mind how the property owners in those neighborhoods will be affected. Never mind that pure logic says this will destroy their property values. It's racism and white privilege to express such ideas!

For those who live in ethnic neighborhoods of their own choosing, being close to family and friends that share traditions and outlooks, it means being forced into neighborhoods where they are not wanted and where they do not want to be. It means a loss of freedom of choice and loss of the right to be secure in their home.

In this day of constant accusations of racism for nearly every act, does no one see the irony of the built-in racism in a regulation that assumes those of certain ethnic origins or economic levels are oppressed and unhappy simply because they live in a different kind of environment than that of the enforcers? What could make them feel more lost and hopeless than to be forced into living in government controlled housing in a neighborhood where they are shunned and resented?

Under AFFH rules, Americans will simply have no choice in the kind of neighborhood in which they wish to live. Using the excuse of equality, HUD- dictated quotas are being enforced. As a result, property values will plummet. Equity in home values will be lost as resale prices fall. Poverty will grow – not diminish -- by these tyrannical rules to reorganize our society.

However, the danger of AFFH goes beyond the destruction of American neighborhoods. It is, in fact, a direct threat to locally elected home rule in communities across the nation. The danger lies in the taking of federal grants. If a community has taken such grants to fund local development, create low income housing programs, and more, then that community has essentially sacrificed its independence to HUD. The fact is, nearly every community has already taken such grants in the name of Smart Growth, Sustainable Development and the creation of Comprehensive Development Plans.

Now, HUD is coming back to collect its due and communities are about to find out there is no such thing as free money. No matter what the city fathers desire for local policy, after taking such grants, HUD will now dictate the use of that money under AFFH rules.

CHAPTER TWENTY-FIVE

THE AMERICAN DREAM FORECLOSED

Meanwhile, in the name of Sustainable Development, the growing tyranny of out-of-control government expands into every segment of our society as innocent people see their lives destroyed and jail cells looming as the bulldozers line up for their assaults on more neighborhoods. Here are just a few more stories of Americans who have personally felt the transformation and suffered its consequences.

» In the city of St. Pete Beach, Florida, the local government filed suit against five residents who said they were opposed to a redevelopment plan officials claim would increase population and tax bases. The residents simply wanted to put the issue on the ballot and let the community decide. City officials sued because they said the state wouldn't allow citizens the right to vote on a redevelopment plan like the one under consideration. Apparently letting people vote wouldn't be sound policy for the common good.

» In Norwood, Ohio, Carl and Joy Gamble stand to lose their home of 35 years so developer Jeffrey Anderson can expand his $500,000,000 empire with a new mall.

» More than 20 homeowners in Long Branch, NJ, many of whom have owned their oceanfront homes for generations, may be kicked off of their land for the construction of expensive condominiums.

» In Riviera Beach, Florida, a predominately black community (and one of the last affordable waterfront neighborhoods in Florida) is threatened by a massive redevelopment plan that may condemn up to 2,000 homes and businesses in favor of more expensive homes, upscale retail, and a yacht club, boat marina and other luxury amenities. Apparently, such luxuries are essential to the common good.

» In downtown Washington, DC, homes were torn down in order to make room for the new Nationals baseball stadium. The new location is only a few miles from the existing RFK stadium, already owned by the city. But the venerable old facility lacked luxury boxes and fancy amenities, so residents' homes had to go and local taxpayers must cough up to fund the new one.

» In Orem, Utah, Betty Perry was arrested, handcuffed, and put in a holding tank because the grass in her front yard was dying. Violation – said the local zoning enforcement officer.

» Julie Bass, in Oak Park, Michigan, wanted to plant an organic garden in her yard. She even asked the Mayor and the City Council if it was okay. Both said yes. But as she went to work on it she, too, was arrested by the local zoning enforcement officer and faced 90 days in jail.

» Power companies, in partnership with government, are now installing smart meters on private homes. These meters give the power company control over the temperature in your home. They will control the thermostat as a means to "cutting your carbon footprint" under the excuse of stopping global warming.

» Across the nation, the FDA is swarming over producers of unprocessed milk, confiscating products, shutting down plants, and arresting producers and buyers alike – even though there have been no reports of sickness or deaths. Not even a complaint.

» In Fauquier County, VA, organic farmer Martha Boneta faced fines of $15,000 a day as her small farm store was closed down. All for holding a children's birthday party on her own land without the proper permit.

These are not the actions of a free society. Americans are guaranteed the right through the Fourth Amendment to the Constitution to be secure in our homes.

As has become obvious on these pages, the problem is not traditional zoning and planning. The problem is the emergence of raw government power that is unchecked and out of control as it ignores individual liberty and private property rights and more government power leads to more government corruption.

Even if you believe there needs to be changes in our society to protect the environment, surely any honest America would admit that such actions by government are out of line.

CHAPTER TWENTY-SIX

THE WALK OF SHAME –
THE NATIONAL ASSOCIATION
OF REALTORS

The National Association of Realtors (NAR) is the mainstream organization in which nearly every real estate agent in the nation belongs as a means to keep up with the latest ideas and trends in the property-selling industry. NAR's members are the professionals that all of us look to for the best approach to buy and sell our homes. One of NAR's mottos is "protecting the American dream of home ownership". And they claim to protect property rights.

Would it then surprise you that NAR is a major promoter of the plan that actually results in the destruction of private property rights? In truth, NAR is a major proponent of Smart Growth.

To promote its Smart Growth policy, NAR paints a delightful, positive picture of a Smart Growth future in its documents: "Our members don't just sell homes, they sell neighborhoods." By promoting Smart Growth, NAR says it's working to "create a range of housing opportunities and choices."

Say NAR Smart Growth materials: "Providing quality housing for people of all income levels is an integral component in any smart growth neighborhood. Housing diversity in terms of type and cost provides a healthy, diverse community. By using smart growth approaches to create a wider range of housing choices, municipalities can reduce the environmental costs of auto-dependent development, use their infrastructure resources more efficiently, ensure better balance of jobs, and housing, and generate a strong foundation of support for neighborhood transit, commercial centers and other services."

Through surveys that have been created to deliver a pre-determined outcome, planners and NAR tell us that 84% of residents believe their communities are getting worse and thus are "demanding" such planning be done to improve things. Under that excuse, NAR is just working hard "through the smart growth strategies to help create the neighborhoods consumers are demanding." And to make it all happen, they are passing out NAR Smart Growth Action Grants to realtor groups all over the nation.

Where do such ideas originate and whom is NAR working with to create such a policy? Well, to begin with, NAR is a member of the Smart Growth Network. It is joined by such organizations as the U.S. Environmental Protection Agency (EPA), Natural Resources Defense Council, American Farmland Trust, Rails to Trails Conservancy, and even the State of Maryland, among others. Now there's a crew from which any promoter of private property rights should run as fast as possible.

Just for the record, the Natural Resources Defense Council (NRDC), founded in 1970, was created by a grant from the Ford Foundation to be an environmental lawfirm. Their favorite tactic is to aggressively sue American industry and state governments to force compliance with radical environmental regulations, costing thousands of jobs and millions of dollars in lost revenues. The American Farmland Trust's method of "preserving" family farms is acquisition and control of development rights, essentially controlling the farms and how they operate. Rails to Trails Conservancy is infamous for taking property that was leased to now defunct railroads and turning the right-of-ways into bike and hiking paths. The only problem is, those pathways are in many cases still owned by the property owners who leased them to the railroads. Basically the trails are pure theft from the property owners. Pretty strange bedfellows for the National Association of Realtors to be playing with.

But, there's more. Throughout the NAR literature on smart growth, it continually quotes the United Nation's World Commission on Environment and Development, better known as the Brundtland Commission. Another UN meeting that led to the findings and suggested policies for development of human society, Habitat I, held in 1976 in Vancouver declared in its official report, "Land cannot be treated as an ordinary asset, controlled by individuals and subject to the pressures and inefficiencies of the market. Private land ownership is also a principle instrument of accumulation and concentration of wealth, and therefore contributes to social injustice."

Wait a minute! Isn't that the very definition of the sale of real estate? Aren't homebuyers individuals seeking to earn wealth from the equity that will be gained by the purchase of the property? Isn't that the very pitch every single realtor in the nation uses to encourage us to buy a home? Why, then would NAR bother to hang around with, and promote policies created by such people? Why would an organization like the National Association of Realtors jump on the bandwagon to support such an anti-people, anti-private property policy? How can such a policy be defended by an organization that says it advocates private property ownership and healthy communities?

The answer to all of those questions is, of course "money and power." The NAR is taking grants to support Smart Growth programs. And in doing so it gets to play with the big boys in Washington, D.C. Why else would the NAR have its national headquarters there?

NAR claims it speaks for all Realtors. If so, then it's past time for America's realtors to stop turning a blind eye to the policies being pro-moted by their national association. Because, in time, as more smart growth policies are forced into place, there will be less and less private property for realtor's to sell. Soon the real estate industry will disappear along with free enterprise, private property and individual choice.

Realtors - for your own survival -- it's time to say no to the socialism of the National Association of Realtors.

CHAPTER TWENTY-SEVEN

WHAT SHALL OUR FUTURE BE? SOLUTIONS

Over the past two and a half decades the policy of Sustainable Development has succeeded in taking over every aspect of society worldwide. It controls energy, water use, and land use from rural areas to cities. It dominates every decision made at every level of government – succeeding in changing the very structure of government. It determines decisions made by private business about products and how they are sold through advertising.

Above all, Sustainable ideology has taken control of the education system, indoctrinating students with one view and one acceptable way to address the issues of life. How are they doing that? By stealing a generation of children and, through the public education system, teaching them to be the perfect global citizens. Today, in the public classrooms, academic education is being replaced with what can only be called indoctrination programs. The process is designed to change the attitudes, values, and beliefs of the children – away from traditional American values of limited government, free enterprise, individual liberty, family, and an American work ethic.

To make the point let those in charge of this change tell you their plans in their own words. Chester Pierce was a professor in the Department of Educational Psychiatry at Harvard University. He was a major architect in the development of the "new" American to reside in the global village. In 1973, Professor Pierce addressed 2,000 teachers attending the International Education Seminar in Denver, Colorado. This was at the beginning of the restructuring of American Education.

He said, "*Every child in America entering school at the age of five is insane because he comes to school with certain allegiances toward our Founding Fathers, toward his parents, toward our elected officials, toward a belief in a supernatural being, and toward the sovereignty of this nation as a separate entity. It's up to you, teachers, to make all of these sick children well by creating the international child of the future.*" Could his intentions be any clearer? Now, over forty years later, we are seeing the results as the youth of the nation stand on the front lines in the fight to transform our society under Sustainable Development. They have no idea of the misery they are now creating for themselves.

Without question, the Forces of Control have managed to find the trick to take over the world without firing a shot. Indeed, they have succeeded in getting the very victims of their conquest to accept that control voluntarily. In fact, they have even succeeded in getting those they've conquered to attack anyone who is trying to stop the assault. Conquered nations are indeed providing the necessary rules, regulations and funding to keep expanding Sustainable control.

Free enterprise. Private property. Individuals. Are these ideas and the freedoms they represent dead in our modern society? If so then Sustainable Development is our future and its proponents our new kings. Our personal actions in accepting or opposing these policies will determine that reality.

Let's not fool ourselves into believing that Sustainable Development is a noble cause. Remember, Sustainable Development was created – not to improve and enrich society – but to reorganize and control it. Its perpetrators have said nothing less. They have openly admitted that its purpose is to change our economic system away from free enterprise. They have stated that private property ownership is racist. And they have attacked the concept of individuality as selfish and a danger to their plans. Harvey Ruvin, a leader of ICLEI USA said, "The individual will have to take a back seat to the collective." Can it be any clearer what they intend for us all? The result can only have one final solution: more poor, fewer choices, disappearing property rights, disappearing jobs -- all leading to more government raging out of control.

In February, 2018, the UN sponsored yet another international conference in Kuala Lumpur, Malaysia, called the World Urban Forum. At this meeting, bureaucrats and NGO representatives from around the world met to plan how to further implement their goals to replace free markets with central planning.

On their schedule for discussion were:

» Regulating businesses to change their profit-motive operations to one "based on the principles of environmental sustainability and inclusive prosperity…(i.e. socialism)

» Creating new rights to government housing and redistribution of wealth.

» Expanding "sexual and reproductive health-care services." (i.e. population control).

» Using cities as a vehicle to transfer great wealth from tax and ratepayers to "green energy" corporations. Already in the U.S. many states are implementing this through a program called Benefit Corporations, basically rewarding any corporations that agree to play ball with the Sustainablists. They get tax-breaks, while consumers get higher prices and fewer choices.

The bottom line is that Sustainable Development fulfills the promise of Socialism. It encourages people to shun personal responsibility, to stop being innovative, and to stop trying to succeed. thus leaving the task to government and thereby making control over us, the masses, a much simpler task. The result is a destroyed society, crashing economy and the complete misery all of that produces.

Sustainable Development control is based on Social Justice. That alone is contrary to American law as Social Justice is rooted in the concept that the accused is guilty until proven innocent. That's because Social Justice isn't based on the rule of law, legal justice, or the use of reason. Rather it's based on emotions. It's the group whine that insists that anyone having more than they need should share it with the less fortunate. It doesn't matter if one became successful from hard work, or an innovative idea that made life better for millions, or one just inherited their wealth from another successful person. Once accused of the crime of success beyond that of others, there is no way to be considered innocent. "It's not fair," is the battle cry. Redistribution of wealth is the goal. And that's how a culture is destroyed, wealth is robbed by the masses, private property is obliterated, and individuals are forced into the collective never to stand out again. That's Sustainable Development.

Consider the results of Sustainable policy so far.

In the rural areas, undertaking any kind of industry which deals with the land and resources is nearly impossible to do. Rules and regulations have been employed to virtually destroy the timber, mining, and ranching industries, all under the excuse of protecting the environment. Yet, isn't it ironic that it's apparently okay, environmentally, to accept imports of timber, minerals and food produced in other nations? Are these nations not on the same planet that the Sustainablists insist must be protected? Obviously the purpose is not the protection of the planet – but redistribution of our national wealth to fund a global system.

Meanwhile, for those still struggling to live in the rural areas, land is systematically locked away from human use through Heritage Areas, wildlife corridors, wetlands regulations, endangered species regulations, water controls, and predator placements such as wolves and bears that destroy livestock and endanger lives. Everyday the amount of land available to human activity shrinks a little more, making it further impossible to live on the rural lands, leaving the residents little choice but to move into approved human habitat areas called Smart Growth.

In the cities, the drive is on to make all cities look and operate exactly alike, destroying individual character as they are ruled from the top-down, eliminating local control, assuring everyone lives the same, earn the same, and think the same. The Sustainablists call these happy, healthy, and diverse communities.

Yet it's vital to note that in these Smart Growth utopias there is a class of people being created that live differently than most of the rest of us – different at least until Sustainable Development policy drives us all to be equally controlled.

We find them in the inner cities. This class is composed of the ethnic, minority, and lower income communities. There you find raw anger, hate, and a growing sense of hopelessness for generations of people. Why? They are the first to feel the full impact of the top-down control of raging government overreach. They are told where to live, how to live, and how much they will be allowed to live on, all dictated to them by government.

Their neighborhoods are the first to be targeted for "improvement" by Smart Growth policies. These are usually established neighborhoods with older buildings, probably in need of improvement and updating. The planners hunger to get their hands on these areas, so they create the grand "vision" for its "improvement," including new buildings, new shopping, new opportunities.

Yet here is the reality. The folks living there are close to their families and life- long friends. Some do own their property, perhaps handed down from older generations. Some own small businesses -- bakeries, restaurants, perhaps even a few operate small manufacturing companies. They aren't getting rich, but they have their own familiar culture, traditions, and way of life; they are comfortable.

Now come the city leaders who see them just as a specific voter block. And THEY have a plan to save these poor, miserable souls from the ravages they have suffered from the unfair, racist system that has kept them down.

The plan is to bulldoze their neighborhoods, destroying their culture, shutting their businesses and wiping out their homes and private property through the power of eminent domain. These entire neighborhoods will be replaced with brand new condos that reach for the sky, complete with corporate stores, restaurants and even offices.

What happens to the people who used to live there? They can't afford these new condos. Ah… the city leaders have a plan for them -- affordable public housing. Those who have lost their jobs or businesses are now forced onto public welfare programs and all is well. They are well taken care of in our Smart Growth utopia.

The fact is the NAACP was partly correct in their suit against Baltimore when they said Section 8 public housing causes ghettos. Throwing whole communities into huge public housing projects naturally creates high crime rates and hopelessness. Desperate people trying to find ways to get ahead usually are given little choice but to turn to crime.

The welfare system in the United States is at fault as it dictates to the recipients that they are not allowed to earn much money or own any business enterprise while in the system or they will lose that government subsidy. So, instead, an underground economy begins to grow. But forced to be underground, that economy is going to be predominately illegal -- drugs, prostitution, stolen goods. Eventually, brutal gangs like MS13 take over the growing crime economy as they threaten and intimidate the locals. Life becomes drudgery and dangerous in the growing blighted areas purposely created by government.

Such is life in the public housing programs where there is hopelessness and despair as these folks see no way out. Government control rather than personal choice and initiative rules the day in more and more neighborhoods in more and more cities as a result of the Smart Growth utopian bulldozers and the weapon called Sustainable Development. That government control was never intended to make these neighborhoods places for the inhabitants to thrive and make something of themselves.

Whether in the rural areas of the nation or in the cities, Sustainable Development's control of the economy, property and individual choice is changing our way of life. Can it be stopped? Is there a way for local communities and their residents to take action to combat it and restore freedom?

The answer is yes, but it will take strong commitment and the ability to think and act creatively and strategically in a unified effort because obviously efforts and tactics used so far haven't worked. Some very courageous and dedicated people have tried to stand in front of the Sustainable juggernaut and stop it. While a few have succeeded to a small extent, most of these efforts have been futile.

Alabama was the first state legislature to actually pass anti-Agenda 21 legislation signed into law by the governor, yet Agenda 21 continues to move forward in that state. Why? Because the legislation failed to define what it meant by Agenda 21. It just talked about the need to disallow the implementation of international policies. It also failed to define the property rights it was intended to protect. The Sustainablists simply said, "Oh, this program isn't international, this is local." And they never used the term Agenda 21, so the evil just charged forward without even slowing down.

Several other states attempted to follow Alabama and pass similar legislation, but the opposition rose up and stopped it. The state of Florida had the best idea when it rescinded legislation that required communities to produce comprehensive development plans. Communities could still do it, but it was no longer required by the state. That was a step in the right direction, but communities continue to fall prey to the NGOs pressure for more projects and more grants. And so, even there, it continues.

One of the most creative and effective tactics used against Sustainable policy was put together in tiny Rindge, New Hampshire. There, the residents began to question policies coming through the county government. At the time, the local folks knew little about Agenda 21 and Sustainable Development, but they understood that new regulations were intrusive and wrong. So a battle began. In the end, the entire county commission was replaced at the ballot box. Most importantly, a resolution was passed making it mandatory that before the county government could apply for a new HUD grant there must first be a vote of the citizens to approve it. However, even in Rindge some of the policies continue to move forward as a result of pressure from federal and state policy, because once a community has taken federal funds the strings are permanent and the feds are unforgiving.

In recent years more than 650 American cities had joined the International Council for Local Environmental Initiatives(ICLEI), paying dues to that Pro-Agenda 21 international NGO so that it could bring in the tools, computer programs, and training to help impose Sustainable programs. As anti-Agenda 21 forces began organizing opposition to

ICELI and more people could clearly see the dangers of this supposedly innocuous program, more than 150 cities dropped their memberships. This was, of course, seen as a positive step forward in stopping Agenda 21. However, a quick check in most of those cities that dropped their memberships will find that the programs continue to move forward for two basic reasons. First, in the face of opposition, it is a typical tactic of the Sustainablists to simply change the names of the programs or redirect them in a different manner, while promoting them as new. ICLEI, for example, rebranded itself to the name Local Governments for Sustainability, then again as Local Action21 (LA21). Each change came about because their actions under the old name were exposed by local freedom-minded individuals and rejected by the people. Second, as was done with the President's Council on Sustainable Development, the programs are embedded into every department of state and local governments, then the program names are removed. So they become invisible, like a cancer lurking in the bone-marrow.

Over the past decade natural disasters have played major roles in the enforcement of Sustainable policies. After Katrina destroyed homes and neighborhoods in New Orleans and Sandy pounded New Jersey, the government process for rebuilding, dictated by federal grants and agency policy is enforcing Sustainable policy calling for more high-rises and public transportation, while placing severe restrictions on rebuilding single-family homes. It will be interesting to watch the process in rebuilding the massive amount of the 2017 fire damage in California. Can property owners stand up to the government's emergency-driven onslaught?

When the American Planning Association organized its "boot camps" to retrain its planners to counter opposition to Sustainable policy their "Glossary for the Public" said, *"Given the heightened scrutiny of planners by some members of the public, what is said – or not said –is especially important in building support for planning."* That's how they hide their true purpose and that's how they continue to sneak the real goals of Sustainable policy past a questioning public.

It's a daunting task to stand up to the Sustainable forces, as they are massively funded and thus powerful. Most of the tactics used so far in fighting back haven't worked because they have all been based on direct confrontation against Agenda 21. The NGOs and planners have done a good job of defeating that opposition simply by labeling it as representing fringe conspiracy theories.

The good (and bad) news, however, is that more and more people now have been affected by these policies. Frankly, the more victims there are the better chance to get the public's attention. That is what is happening across the nation. Many elected officials are taking notice of the intrusion by federal agencies, such as HUD, EPA and DOT against their local governmental responsibilities. Some of these local officials are starting to ask questions and seek answers as to how to stop it.

So now is the time for the American public to either stand up and stop this massive transformation of our society, or watch as the Sustainable Development rat-hole opens up and swallows us.

A NEW STRATEGY TO STOP SUSTAINABLE DEVELOPMENT

To stop Agenda 21/Sustainable Development will take an entirely new strategy over what has been employed so far. No longer can citizens just stand in opposition to Agenda 21. The proponents always counter with "so what's your solution?" They ask this in confidence, knowing that they have already laid the groundwork for creating a crisis that must now be solved… "somebody must do something." So now, if opponents simply come back with "it's against the Constitution," "it's my property," or "this is a UN policy," the officials' eyes will roll and such opposition will be dismissed without comment.

Instead, opposition must offer positive, non-governmental, free-market, real solutions that offer hope, the promise of a future and a life of one's own. It must be a strategy of small but effective steps applied, especially on the local and state levels where opposition is more directly discerned than is possible on the national level. Of course, there must also be an effort to counter federal policy and dictates. However, a concentrated, successful effort locally will have a strong effect on state policy. Eventually, with enough success on local and state levels, federal policy will begin to be affected as well, just as the nation's founders intended.

I hope, through this book, that I've made one fact perfectly clear – Sustainable Development cannot be enforced without destroying private property rights. So the most effective way to combat it is to wage an all out political battle to protect and preserve property rights from the rural areas to the inner cities.

Let's detail a new, positive, solution that doesn't call for new governmental programs, rather a roll-back of government intrusion. And let's show how a coordinated effort of local and state elected officials, combined with citizen activists and business can bring about a true freedom-oriented transformation to our nation.

CHAPTER TWENTY-EIGHT

AN AGENDA TO RESTORE PROPERTY RIGHTS

Across the nation there are pockets of dedicated activists and elected officials who are valiantly fighting in their local city councils, county commissions, and state legislatures. But in most cases they are outnumbered, out spent, out maneuvered, and overpowered by the Sustainablists and their hordes of NGO operatives. It can feel very hopeless to stand alone in the fight, especially when suffering defeat after defeat. It's time to start pooling resources and fighting smarter and more effectively. Here is a very brief outline of actions to be taken to organize an effective opposition.

First action is to organize a network of such grassroots activists and officials where they can network, share ideas, and communicate using the Internet, YouTube, and other social media. Establish a central webpage where all can post their experiences and share their victories and defeats for everyone to learn what works and what doesn't. This group should be expanded to include pastors, and non-political residents who find themselves victims of Sustainable policies. In addition, reach out to local businesses and corporations that advocate helping small business. They each have a legitimate interest in the outcome and can be invaluable in reaching out to local and state government. This is how you build a movement.

Create a committee of a few dedicated activists who will commit to attending every council meeting and every planning session, take notes and report to the coalition new developments in order to prepare opposition or support, as needed. Create a second committee that deals with the media, public relations and social media to broadcast the details of these local plans. Make an effort to get members of your coalition onto planning and advisory boards so that your voice is heard. Always be prepared to speak out. Never attempt to fight alone. Ten dedicated people can make a huge difference. One person, acting alone, can be made to look like a fringe loon.

When speaking in opposition to plans, don't rudely shout down those officials who are proposing them. Instead, do your homework and present well-informed, researched facts, supporting data, and examples of other jurisdictions that were forced to comply with similar regulations and share the results. Then ask the officials to do their own research to see if you aren't right. This can help you take the high ground and appear the reasonable ones in the debate. It can help you gain allies, both with citizens and perhaps some of the officials.

Most importantly, begin to target elected officials who are promoting and supporting Smart Growth programs and land grabs. Make them feel pain – meaning expose them to the public, make them accountable for their actions and vote them out of office whenever possible -- making sure you have a candidate to carry your message against them. It is a guarantee that, if only one or two members of the local government are pushed out of office as a result of their supporting and imposing Sustainable Development policy, you will have the attention of the rest of those on elective boards and therefore have a better chance to stop them. Fear of your opposition is a powerful tool. Make all elected officials feel very uncomfortable in dealing with the outsider NGOs. Help them to understand that it's not free.

IN THE STATE LEGISLATURES

State legislators have much more power than they may realize. They can block federal edicts and refuse to obey them. The Constitution, in its clearly written enumeration of powers, specifically states what the federal government may do. All other decisions are up to the states. It's called the Tenth Amendment. One of the main reasons our nation is suffering from an out-of-control national government is because the states have forgotten, ignored, or surrendered their powers and have allowed the federal government to dictate to them. To stop Sustainable Development the states must take back their rightful responsibilities.

Even if anti-Sustainable, pro-limited government legislators are in a minority they can effectively impact the legislative process. First, such like-minded legislators must form a tight coalition to work together under a Freedom Agenda Pledge:

"I solemnly pledge to my constituents that I will consistently vote to defund, or vote against appropriating money for any state participation in the implementation or enforcement of an federal regulatory program or activity not specifically authorized by an enumerated power in the United States Constitution because when such program or activity is not specifically authorized by an enumerated power it is not allowed under the United States Constitution. For any State participation I do vote to fund, I will provide the specific enumerated power constitutionally permitting it."

Legislators should establish a ten-year plan to outline their legislative goals defining where they want the state government to stand in ten years, then begin to create very comprehensive, all-inclusive legislative plans to achieve those goals. Next, take this legislation and break it down into small individual bills to pass one at a time rather than attempting to pass a single one-size-fits-all bill, (that has been tried several times, but only succeeds in bringing out the pro-Sustainable forces en masse to defeat it).

Dividing it up into small bills, perhaps focusing on just a specific violation of property rights will help ease opposition. For example easing restrictions on enforcing comprehensive plans or offering a five-year opt out on conservation easements will make it difficult for the Sustainablists to build major opposition. In support, the argument can be made that the sky isn't falling, these bills don't stop comprehensive plans or conservation easements, instead, they are simply giving local governments and property owners a choice.

Attack, Attack, Attack every effort by the pro-Sustainablists. Do not give an inch on your principles. As your guide for opposing or supporting legislation, use the SCRAP Test. Does the bill increase the Size, Cost, Reach And Power of government? If so –**SCRAP** it.

In addition, even though such legislators may be a minority in their state body, the movement can grow and sound legislation can spread by reaching out to like-minded legislators in other states. Communicate, coordinate, and take direct action. Imagine the impact if members in ten state legislators dropped the same bills into their respective legislative hoppers on the same day, each holding a news conference to announce it. That gives it a powerful start with major publicity. Then, if multiple states pass such specific legislation to roll back government it will catch fire and become a movement in more states, eventually becoming a vital agenda. Above all, be determined in all legislative actions to take back control of the legitimate government and end the tyrannical assault of the top-down control agenda of Sustainable Development.

IN LOCAL GOVERNMENT

City Councils and County Commissions are the best places to organize to stop the Sustainable invasion. This is where you may have a personal relationship with an elected representative and where you can have the most influence. But you must not try to exercise that opposition alone. This is where your coalition must be organized, educated about the issues, and prepared with a goal and a plan to achieve it.

Have you ever wondered why your elected officials always seem to be susceptible and even eager to impose these plans? Have you wondered why they refuse to listen to your opposition? Well, for the answer, you need to fully understand and see the true makeup of your local government. It's not just the five or seven council members or county commissioners. And it's also more than just the NGOs and the planners.

Of course there are the typical NGOs like the Sierra Club and a host of others representing individual issues like bike lanes, land trusts, energy and water issues, historic preservation, and housing development, for example. Each brings their own well-worn plan and the application for the individual grants to see them enforced. And of course there are several different planning groups like the American Planning Association.

However there is another line of heavy influence standing behind all of these layers of your hidden government. People who run for our local and state offices are not necessarily evil or wrongheaded. In many cases they are just good people who want to serve their community. However, when we elected our city councils, county commissions, mayors, legislators and governors, almost every community does a strange thing with these new, eager leaders. We send them off to indoctrination centers. Of course, they aren't officially called that. Here are some examples.

U.S. Conference of Mayors: Elect a new mayor and send him/her off to this national meeting where he/she can meet with other mayors and share and gain ideas for the community. That's a good idea, right? After all, this is an official government organization where our mayor should be.

Well, the U.S. Conference of Mayors is actually a 501(c)(3) private organization whose member cities are those with populations over 30,000. In 1996 they made the UN's Kyoto Global Warming Treaty a centerpiece of the Conference's agenda – calling on all cities to use the provisions of the treaty to reduce their carbon footprint. In addition, the Conference of Mayors has accepted the UN's Earth Charter as a guideline for policy decisions.

National Association of Counties: A private, 501(c)(3) organization, County Commissioners are sent here where 50 state affiliates represent more than half of the counties in America. Together with the U.S. Conference of Mayors, the Association of Counties established the Joint Center for Sustainable Communities and then provided the framework for Bill Clinton's Presidential Council on Sustainable Development.

National League of Cities: a private 501(c)(3) organization, the League of Cities represents more than 1,400 dues-paying communities. The League supports gun control, and opposes any kind of restrictions on state governments' takings of private land.

National Conference of State Legislatures: A 501(c)(3) private organization which works to ensure that federal programs operate hand-in-hand with state programs, making sure that federal programs are implemented into state policy in a seamless or harmonized manner – making it easier to argue that such polices are state rather than federal – its all local!

Council of State Governments: a private 501(c)(3) organization. The Council promotes worldwide "sustainable" zoning and such uniform state codes and regulatory systems, providing model statues for legislatures.

National Governors Association: A private 501(c)(3) organization that advocates Smart Growth, more government benefits for illegals, worked to block workfare requirements for welfare benefits and supports taxing the Internet.

These are the organizations to which we send our newly elected officials to learn about the proper role of government. As they listen to speaker after speaker we find that these are most likely the NGOs and planners, sharing program ideas and building the dream, all leading to Sustainable Development. The officials are even given sample legislation to take home. When they arrive home, the officials are met with representatives from the same NGO groups ready to help them put the policies in place. And, of course, they are armed with the grants to fund it all. Eventually, your elected representatives begin to believe this is all the proper role of government. So when local activists come in to oppose such plans, their immediate reaction (supported by the NGOs) is that you are fringe nuts to be ignored.

Of course, all of this is backed by these "official" leagues and associations that are obviously "official branches of government." So if they say it's the right thing to do, obviously it is! There's just one problem with that impression. All of these groups are 501(c)(3) private organizations. They are NOT governmental or mandatory. They have private agendas and membership by your community or attendance by your elected officials is not mandatory. The only reason these organizations, including the NGOs and planners, have any influence or power in your community is because your elected officials give it to them. Begin a campaign to end your community's or state's membership in these private organizations, and above all, work to stop your officials from attending their indoctrination meetings.

Knowing that your elected officials are under this kind of pressure and influence, how do you combat it? Of course, the local level is where the NGOs and planners mass behind your officials. Here they supply the tools, the training, and the money to make it all happen. A little research will reveal who the NGOs are. But before you attempt to go after them, be sure to organize your committee that is responsible for attending all of the council sessions as well as the planning meetings. Take note of who is in attendance. This will give you insight into the NGOs and planners. It will be obvious that several people in the room don't appear to be local, yet they seem to wield strong influence. You may see your local officials deferring to them during the meetings. These may be planners, NGO representatives, or perhaps even federal agents from HUD, EPA or DOT. Study them and find out who they are. You need to know who and what is to be your opposition.

The first order of business in your fight is to stop the local government from taking the federal grants. The NGOs are pushing them hard behind closed doors. Your voice will seem out of place and a bit crazy to your officials. Why not take the "free" money?" This is where your research team will become vital. They can provide research to show why it isn't "free." It's vital that elected officials be made aware of the implications and the hidden strings attached to the grants. Plan your attacks accordingly.

Make the center of your attacks based on protecting private property rights. Go through each program and "visioning" plan prepared for the community. For each regulation ask the question about how property rights will be protected. Carefully document each response from the officials. At first they will assure you that property rights will, of course, be protected. Some will assure you they are property owners too, and so they can be trusted to protect their own interests as well as yours. Ask them if they are willing to put that in writing! As the NGOs are flipping out behind them over that question, the officials will quickly refuse.

An activist, in Pickens County, South Carolina, Johnnelle Raines, fought a tremendous battle in her county commission attempting to get them to agree to protect property rights as they brought in the plans and planners. She presented them with a Resolution for the Protection of Citizens Property Rights that asked for three provisions in writing: 1. That, if the county and planners were going to discuss projects that would affect a citizen's property then the citizen would be brought in to the discussion. 2. If the country decided to move forward and the plan would affect the citizen's property monetarily, the county would compensate the owner. 3. That the county could not bring planners and other government representatives onto a citizen's property for planning and measuring without the owner's permission. Nothing radical there. Just commons sense property rights protection.

Yet, immediately the county attorney took Johnnelle's resolution and began to mark it up, expressing how impossible it would be to make such promises. But she kept pressing, demanding answers. Finally she go it. They state that the South Carolina Constitution did not provide protection for private property from seizure by government or even private companies. "*At present, private property may only be taken for 'public use,' for example, to build a road or to construct a public building. But the state constitution doesn't define public use, with the result that state laws may be passed by the legislature and upheld by the court that allow government to take land for almost any reason at all.*"

There you have it, your local government hiding behind a lack of definition to refuse to protect private property. Did the county attorney or a single member of the county commission take the time to contact a state legislator to point out this lack of definition and ask them to correct the problem? No. To do so would somehow serve to diminish the power of government and so is not to be considered. Such is the mindset of government under Sustainable Development.

Here is a perfect opportunity for an activist network, working with like-minded elected officials to start a drive to force a campaign for property rights definition and protection in each state.

Above all, such cowardly officials, afraid to step out of the shadows of the NGOs who rule them, must be made examples. A group of ten or twenty-five dedicated activists can make this happen. First, to force the issue, a dedicated and brave activist like Johnnelle, who selflessly took the lead in the fight, should have been supported by ten people behind her ready to protest this lame excuse by the county government. They needed to attend every meeting asking **why** the council won't take action to protect property rights. More needed to be out in front of the county building with signs containing the pictures of the Commissioners, asking **why** they won't protect property rights. Make it personal – because taking your property is a very personal thing! Make them feel pain and responsibility for their actions! And finally, put up a candidate who will make the growing protest the center of his campaign to oust the cowards! Do you think my language is too offensive? Then just wait until it's your property they have taken. These are necessary actions that must be imposed to take back your community. By the way, "**why**" is the most radical question in the English language! Ask it often.

IN THE RURAL AREAS

All of the above also must be done in the rural areas as well as in the cities. In addition, there are issues specific and unique to rural areas that need to be addressed.

Without question the western states have been set up for such control by government. The Founders intended for property to be privately owned in each state, except in specific cases of government need, such as roads, government buildings, and forts, as outlined in Article 1, section 8 of the Constitution. However, beginning in the 1930s, the federal government began what can only be described as an assault on private ownership in the western states. In 1934 Congress passed the Taylor Grazing Act and created the U.S. Grazing Service to manage livestock grazing on public lands. While the act indicated grazing was to last until Congress disposed of the lands, it was the first time the federal government had authorized direct management of state lands and had been freely available for use by local ranchers. In 1946, the General Land Office and the U.S Grazing Service were merged to form the Bureau of Land Management (BLM). Its job was to now review public land policy and determine how it should be controlled or perhaps disposed – whichever would achieve maximum benefit for the general public. Finally, in 1976, the Federal Land Policy and Management Act was passed, stating that the federal government should retain ownership unless disposal of the property would serve the national interest.

This was the process that has led to the biggest government land-grab in the nation's history. Specifically, huge amounts of land are now under the control of the federal government instead of the states. This is the reason why the West was the first target of the Sustainablists. There was simply nothing to stand in their way. Ranchers operating on those "public lands" don't have legal deeds, as in the east. Instead they were given assurances of grazing rights and water rights – on public lands. This made it easy for federal agencies like the EPA and Bureau of Land Management (BLM) to ignore such legal rights for the use of the land (that have been proven time and again in court to be legitimate guarantees). Of course, the tactic of Social Justice has also been employed to replace law with emotion, allowing the BLM to exercise control, confiscated cattle and levy fines as it sees fit, because it "belongs to the people." To reverse this massive federal control, affected States must demand a reversal of these policies and reestablish their state sovereignty rather than federal control over the lands inside their boundaries, as it is in every eastern state.

In other rural areas of the nation, states must begin to reign in the land trusts that are busy taking private property through control of Conservation Easements. It is absolute insanity to allow these land trust to force control over rural lands and farms "in perpetuity." That's forever! Yet, the land trusts don't have to keep them that long. They, in fact, are able to buy, sell and trade these easements among other land trusts and with the federal government. Such actions are a major source of revenue for land trusts like the Nature Conservancy. As a result, the landowner is never sure who controls the easement and what new rules may appear. It would be fair, as mentioned earlier, to allow the landowner some of the same freedom as the land trusts. State legislatures need to provide a five-year opt out for the landowners. That is plenty of time for the landowner to learn if the easement is going to work for them.

Another favorite trick of the land trusts involves collusion with federal agencies to take private land. Here's an example of how one of the nation's largest land trusts, the Nature Conservancy, profits from the land grab game:

» Your grandmother owns land close to a historic site or a wilderness area. The government wants the land to expand a park, but grandmother won't sell. One day a representative of the Nature Conservancy shows up at her door. He's well dressed, smiling – but concerned. He tells your grandmother that he's just learned that the government intends to take her land after she passes away. She won't be able to sell it or leave it to her children. However, he can offer a solution.

» If grandmother will sell her land to the Nature Conservancy he can assure her that the land will stay in private hands and not be taken by the government. Whew, a relieved grandmother is much happier and she agrees to sell. However, says the nice man from the Nature Conservancy, because the government intends to take the land, its value is now only about half of its previous market value. And so that's all he'll be able to pay her. Half. Well, thinks grandmother, half is better than nothing, so she sells.

» The next day, our friend from the Nature Conservancy makes a call to the Department of Interior informing them that their plan to get the land has worked. The whole thing had been prearranged between them before anyone ever knocked on grandmother's door. As arranged, the Nature Conservancy will now sell the land to the Department of Interior FOR THE FULL MARKET VALUE – PLUS OVERHEAD COSTS, FINANCING, AND HANDLING CHARGES.

So, if ever you receive a knock on the door from a smiling representative of the Nature Conservancy (or any land trust) slam it in his face and rush to your neighbors to sound the alarm, or the saying "there goes the neighborhood" could take on a completely different meaning.

Sustainable farming is another threat to small farmers. It's designed for corporate farms that play ball with the Sustainablists while the higher costs caused by such regulations destroy small farms. Small farms have been feeding the nation for over two hundred years. They know full well that the land must be protected or they will be out of business. Massive environmental regulations imposed by people armed with a political agenda rather than a working knowledge of farming must be pushed back.

The Endangered Species Act is nothing more than another weapon to control land and industry. The Act is used to block development simply by the adding of another, usually rarely heard of insect, fish, mouse, owl, rat, or bat, to the endangered list, simply to block the plowing of a field, building of an airport runway, a hospital or a road which is suddenly discovered to be hidden habitat. Once announced there is very little chance such projects can ever move forward. Yet, in truth, there is very little scientific evidence that the ESA has ever saved a species. To roll back the outrageous control of the federal government the ESA must be repealed.

These and many such schemes are all part of the enforcement of Sustainable Development, designed to control the land and determine who stays and who goes. State legislatures must begin to address such issues, specifically by taking action to protect private property.

SAVING THE INNER CITY

No area in America has suffered more from government overreach that the poor and ethnic neighborhoods of our cities. Rendered powerless by their poverty they have become pawns in the ruthless drive for control, especially useful in promoting the Social Justice scare tactics by the Sustainablists.

As mentioned earlier, these are the people who experience a different America from the rest of society, they are controlled as to where and how they may live, and are kept from working and getting ahead if they are already on government welfare programs. In short, they are the perfect example of where the entire nation is headed if Sustainable polices are allow to be fully implemented. Let us all take a strong lesson from that.

The nation's welfare system promises to provide a lifeline, instead it's a trap. The nation used to provide what was called Assistance. Many times people find themselves just a little short where a couple hundred dollars would fill the gap and help get the bills paid while the recipient works a job for the majority of their income.

That has changed. Today, there is the welfare system that demands that recipients have little or no other means of income to continue receiving its benefits. In addition, recipients can't have a savings account or any other kind of asset that might provide income. To keep getting the welfare check those assets are basically confiscated. Ronald Reagan, as a candidate for President used to tell the story of the woman who was receiving welfare, and, even though it was a very small amount, she was able to put a few dollars away each check. When the government discovered she had such a savings, it was confiscated and she lost her welfare benefits.

In such a system there is absolutely no incentive to even try to get ahead, for every such action becomes a threat to your ability to survive. The only way to get ahead is to work the system which rewards one for having multiple illegitimate children, each bringing in an extra check or operating in an underground economy such as selling drugs, prostitution, or perhaps dealing in stolen goods.

Black leaders such as author Clarence Mason Weaver, author of the book *It's Ok to Leave the Plantation* and Star Parker, head of CURE, each have said the destruction of the black community was the enforcement of government intervention in their lives, under the excuse of saving them from poverty. The result has been more poverty, the destruction of their family units, more crime, less hope.

Most recently their neighborhoods have become the targets of the eminent domain bulldozers of Smart Growth as their homes and businesses are destroyed and more are forced onto the government programs and into government housing projects, there to find more crime and more hopelessness. Is it any wonder there is such rage and hatred exploding from those government created ghettos?

Of course, they must live in fear that even this government promise can be taken away. That's why they instantly and physically react when any politician mentions the economic insanity of the program and the need to cut it back. Get a job, they are told. But who has the courage to voluntarily take themselves off the programs as they dare attempt to get a job with no safety net? With no experience in such a free enterprise situation, they simply can't imagine doing it. Of course the Social Justice warriors take advantage and feed that fear, teaching them that such plans to cut back on the programs are a threat to their existence and, of course, racist.

It's only fair, say the Social Justice warriors, that people should be allowed to live in the better neighborhoods even though they can't afford it, never mind that the very imposition of the public housing rules in upscale areas is the death to their property values for all those folks have worked hard to build. Sound economics have never been a concern of the Social Justice destroyers. Of course the end result is eventually there will be more and more poor as such government tyranny destroys personal investment opportunities. And the hate grows as culture is destroyed.

What can be done to change this situation? Is the hopelessness incurable? What possible government action could be taken to change the direction of this downward plunge for so many people? Worse, unless a solution can be found, it's going to grow as Sustainable Development takes ever greater control of society, the economy, and property.

What if the solution for the inner city, isn't a government program, but instead, a roll back of them – getting government out of the way so that all of these people can make free choices for their own lives and build futures of their own choosing? Is there a way to fix the situation by allowing these neighborhoods to heal themselves and rise to prosperity on their own without a government program?

Former President Ronald Reagan said, "The answer to poverty is freedom and personal responsibility, not a welfare state." As wise men have taught throughout the ages, "Feed a man and he eats for a day, teach him to fish and he feeds himself." HUD Secretary Dr. Ben Carson said, "We need to understand what true compassion is… It's not compassion to pat them on the head and say, 'there, there, I'm going to take care of all your needs, your health care, your food.' That's the opposite of compassion. I'm not interested in getting rid of a safety net. I'm interested in getting rid of dependency."

In those three quotes lies the answer to saving the inner cities from the ravages of government control as imposed by Sustainable Development. Push back government intrusion and allow a free market, property rights and individual choice to rebuild the neighborhoods instead of eminent domain bulldozers.

Of course, the Sustainablists will yell bloody murder over such a suggestion. "Racist!" "An outrageous attempt to bring White Privilege solutions to people who don't have the means to help themselves!" Translation: "We have no intention of taking our foot off these people's throats and letting them have lives of their own!"

The fact is there are all kinds of tools, individuals, and private companies generously wanting to help – if government will just get out of the way and let them do it. HUD Director Carson has stated several times that the answer is not government, but private citizens free to take control of their own lives instead of relying on government dependency. The first step necessary for freeing the folks in the inner cities is for his own agency to begin to back off, ending the tyranny of the Affirmatively Furthering Fair Housing program -- either ending its grant program all together, or at least taking the severe Sustainable strings off of them and reducing compliance restrictions. Let cities that take the grants use them as needed locally, not as dictated federally.

Americans are a very generous people, ready to help those in need, if they themselves aren't taxed to the point of suffocation themselves. The nation used to have a near unlimited number of service organizations like Kiwanis, Lions, Optimists, Exchange Club, Pilot Club, Jay Cees, and many, many more, all volunteers who provided services to acquire such things as eyeglasses, food, housing, medical care, and much more for those in need. Over the years, many of the projects that these groups ran voluntarily, funded by donations, have been taken over by government with its rules and regulations. Slowly these private groups had to give up their own projects, in some cases the groups just ceased to exist. There are still operations like the Shriners Hospital and St. Judes Children's Hospital, which provide free care to families through voluntary donations. Such operations are successful models, if, again, government gets out of the way. Using these models, free of government intrusion, there is no reason for anyone in this nation to be without healthcare. Volunteer organizations to help the truly needy are the answer – not government programs that steal individual choice in the name of compassion from the compassion cartel that needs poverty to flourish so they can grow.

In addition, there are private legal foundations like Institute for Justice that take up the cause for those fighting government overreach that can help lay the legal groundwork for forcing government to back off and begin to build the ability of private citizens in the inner city to once again own and control private property. These legal groups can work hand in hand with certain civil rights groups like the Congress on Racial Equality (CORE) and Star Parker's CURE, both of which have a strong record of recognizing real civil rights causes verses Social Justice scare tactics. More importantly, these groups know that welfare is a trap, not a solution.

Most significantly, private enterprise is vital to the rebuilding of these neighborhoods. There are several associations of small business that promote creating and supporting small business. A main ingredient for building small business in these areas is financing. There are several banks, including BB&T that promote loans for small business. The creation of locally or individually owned bakeries, restaurants, beauty and nail shops, even local manufacturing companies, would erase the need for Smart Growth revitalization projects. Instead the neighborhoods would be restored on their own by the people who live there, just as they were originally built. And that would allow the local residents to create real diversity and neighborhood character from their own ethnic backgrounds and histories, rather than the made-up, mythical – and often unworkable -- kind imposed by government.

Two specific actions are necessary by government to allow these voluntary ideas to move forward and begin to build an "above-ground" economy in the inner cities. First, a reduction in taxes and fees charged by federal, state, and local governments must take place. Second, eliminate unwarranted and unjustified licensing for nearly every business action. These make it nearly impossible for low-income people to ever consider starting a business, even if they have proven products and expertise in the field. Start up fees just for the privilege of starting a company is a tool of large corporations and big government to control who can have a business. Let the people start the business and government will benefit greatly though new taxes and jobs the business will create. And why is it necessary to pay for a license to polish nails? Of course - "Safety!" goes the cry. Customers in a free market will better decide such things with their patronage rather than a government bureaucrat filling out a form.

Finally, folks who have been forced to live on government programs, perhaps for generations, certainly do need a lift to understand how to work a job, show up daily, and take responsibility. There are private organizations that have been created to help in that training. These are generally run by people who come from the inner city, sometimes they are church groups. They raise their funds through private sources. They are better equipped than government to know the local situation and the needs for more effective training. In addition to these training programs, perhaps running hand in hand with them, are entrepreneurs and private investors looking to build new businesses. They provide the start up funds and the training to run them, and then the jobs come. In fact, the 2017 tax bill passed by Congress has a provision called Qualified Opportunity Zones (Subchapter Z) in which private investors receive deferred taxes or tax breaks for investing in low income areas. That can be a powerful new tool to get private investors into these neighborhoods, instead of federal grant money that comes with powerful job killing dictates.

All of these pieces and parts are voluntary, with private money, and they all exist today. Most don't try to take action in the inner cities because of the rules, regulations, taxes, and most of all, the looming bulldozers of Smart Growth. Why bother if it's all going to be torn down eventually? That's the tragedy the poor and underprivileged live with every day. It doesn't have to be that way.

The Sustainablists will argue that those in the inner cities not only don't have the means to take these actions, but they don't have the desire or even an understanding of such thing, and certainly are not ready to take on so much responsibility. Those claims are not only false, but if one wants to bring racism into the argument, I would state that such a position is probably the most racist of all.

Over the past year I have traveled the nation and whenever possible have discussed this kind of free-market solutions with folks living in such conditions. Their responses to these ideas have been universally positive.

Here is an example of one those discussions. I was in New York City at an event specifically to talk with representatives of major media, to pitch my property rights ideas for possible interviews for their programs and publications. The setting for the event was in a ballroom at a hotel in downtown Manhattan, directly across from Madison Square Garden. There were large windows in the room that ran from floor to ceiling. Outside was the massive city of New York. I found myself pitching my ideas to a black radio host for CBS Radio New York. As I was talking to him, suddenly I stopped and said, "look out that window." He turned and looked out over New York. I said, "In all of those buildings there are people paying mortgages and property taxes. But as far as your eyes can see, there is not a single private property right, because someone else is making all of the decisions about that property behind closed doors. And," I added, "only big corporations can own and control property in such a situation, all in partnership with the controlling government." He turned to me with a smile on his face and said, "We've got to get you on my show!" In short, he got what I was saying and was excited about it.

Second Example: I was on a flight to Indiana. The flight attendant on the small plane was a sharp young black man. As it turned out, his jump seat for take-offs and landings was right next to mine. During takeoff he sat down and I started a conversation, asking how he was enjoying his job. He was quite proud and excited about it and the success it was bringing him. Of course, he then asked the inevitable question that always comes up in such conversations, he asked "What do you do?"

I told him I worked to protect people's property rights from government overreach and takings. His response almost knocked me out of my seat. Immediately he said, "How does that affect the displacement of folks in the inner cities?"

Wow, he got it right away! I said, "Yes, that's a major part of the fight!"

He said, "you are doing important work!" Three times during the flight as he passed me he said, keep it up, you are doing important work!"

Such are the responses I have gotten from the black community for these ideas. They want freedom. They want a life of their own and they want a chance to achieve it. They want the opportunity to live normal American Dream lives. All of that is contrary to what is reported by the news and Sustainable politicians who need them to all remain victims under government controlled victimhood.

Private property ownership builds personal wealth and freedom. It will save the inner city, and ultimately it will stop the drive to transform our society from the power-mongers of Sustainable Development.

CHAPTER TWENTY-NINE

RISE AND RISE AGAIN
UNTIL LAMBS BECOME LIONS

Sustainable Development is an international scheme for total control over human society that comes disguised as scores of national and local policies. It is a war against free enterprise, private property and the individual. Sustainable policy is designed to rein in those radical ideas, and to "harmonize" all nations into a central, global control.

Today there is great danger that Americans will accept the sales pitch that Sustainable Development is just a new and better way to organize our communities as simple suggestions on how to protect the environment. All levels of governments are falling for that pitch and are gleefully helping put it in place. If that continues it will be a short step to allow the power-mongers to fully succeed in their goal to change and control our system of government and totally transform our society. Their success can only lead to a Dark Ages across the nation and around the globe, unlike anything ever experienced in human existence. Free thought, free movement, and free exchanges by the people will be a thing of the past. Like the folks now living in the inner cities, and many trying to survive on the nation's ranches, the hopelessness of life will set in. But this time it will be completely devastating for the entire population.

The positive news is that it's not too late to fight. I've tried to give the reader a full understanding of the threat and positive ways to combat it. But you must understand – the fight starts on the local level, not in Washington, DC. Nameless, faceless bureaucrats wielding power in the backrooms, untouchable and unseen, do not represent freedom.

Those forces pushing the Sustainable agenda are deeply entrenched in every city. They are highly organized and massively funded. And they have a very specific goal. They intend to see it fulfilled and will stop at nothing to achieve it. We have one choice – fight. Fight for your homes. Fight for your community. Fight for your very right to exist. It will take political trench warfare in every city council meeting and in every county commission meeting to behead this beast.

One fact is clear – they will not be able to enforce Sustainable Development without eradicating property rights. Private property ownership and its unrestricted use is the foundation for a nationwide revolution of Freedom. Demand it! Stand up for property rights and we can stop sustainable development and put the cork back on government growth. But we need leaders who understand and will act on protecting property rights, without which we have no freedoms. That's where the need for activism comes in. It's time that we demand a government that treats property owners like OWNERS – not chattel to be pushed around as they like. Make defense of private property your battle cry.

First we must understand the nature of the threat we face. Sustainable Development ignores the warnings of John Locke, that the abolition of private property rights will lead to the destruction of human incentive to build, prosper, and succeed on one's own. Instead it would create a society of thieves who live by taking the fruits of the labor of others.

The fact is, Sustainable policy is a political movement led by those who seek to control the economy, dictate development and redistribute wealth. They use the philosophical base of Karl Marx, the tactics of Adolph Hitler, and the rhetoric of the Sierra Club. Basically everything connected with Sustainable Development translates to higher costs, shortages and sacrifice; there is no positive aspect of Sustainable Development.

The danger is in the process! Sustainability policies are being forced on unsuspecting citizens using the Saul Alinsky tactic of creating false hope for the middle class. These are lies that use pre-determined outcomes and group manipulation tactics to force their way into local policy.

The battle will not be won overnight or even in one battle. It will take time and hard work. But the result will be a rock-solid foundation on which to rebuild the hopes and dreams and self-determination for generations.

We who oppose Agenda 21 frankly don't accept the premise that we must destroy our human civilization in order to protect the environment. We believe in free markets and free societies where people make their own decisions, and develop their own property. And we fully believe that the true path to a strong protection of the environment is through private property ownership and limited government.

Those who promote Agenda 21 do not believe in those ideals. Thus, we will not, cannot agree on the path to the future. In short, our fight is a clash of the age-old philosophy of life -- Freedom to live as you choose -- or control by an unseen elite. There is no room for middle ground.

Our greatest problem in fighting is fear. The threat is overwhelming. How to you fight back against such a behemoth? How can you possibly make a difference?

As I think about the suffering Americans have been through over the past few decades as government has spiraled out of control and our culture has changed because of the assault of Sustainable Development, I'm reminded of another time in history. It was also a time when human suffering occurred at the hands of a tyrannical government.

In Thirteenth century England, the king had all the power. He could take property at will. He could tax at any rate he pleased, and in fact claim any possession as his right. He controlled the army, the court system, and every public action was under his purview. He was ruthless in his use of such power and wielded it at his whim. How could the people possibly stand up to such an all-powerful king who was ordained to rule from birth?

However, the human desire for freedom is strong. Even as one pretends to comply, private thoughts and desires are impossible to control, even by an all-powerful force. To do nothing assured defeat and permanent enslavement. Slowly, small acts of defiance took place. Quietly, secret movements began. Every small action worked to inspire another. Then another. More joined the cause until it finally became open rebellion. Quietly, diligently, they organized. Those who had, at one time, been too timid to fight for what was theirs, finally began to understand they had no other choice. The king's tyranny would never go away on its own. A rallying cry became "Rise and Rise Again, Until Lambs Become Lions." That's when the resistance began to finally take hold and eventually forced the king to submit and restore freedom.

Today, Americans, for the first time since becoming a nation, face the same tyranny those Englishmen faced so long ago. We are so used to living in freedom that we aren't sure what to do with such a threat as we now face. The Sustainable enemy is so secretive and subversive many don't even realize our very survival as a free people is at stake and, when told, refuse to believe it. So we must take a lesson from those in our long past history who eventually realized that the only way out was to take action, risking everything.

Play for keeps. Don't concede a single point when dealing with principle. Start on the local and state levels to change things there. If we can preserve freedom in our communities and our states, we can protect it as a nation. The future of freedom depends on your commitment to preserve it.

Sustainable Development is certainly the comprehensive blueprint for the reorganization of human society and it has already invaded every corner of our lives. But the fight to stop it is not hopeless! Stop looking down in defeat and frustration. When our founders created this nation, they were not thinking just of themselves. They were thinking of us, two hundred years in their future. We must now do the same. Think of the future of our children, grandchildren and their children and grandchildren. Will they even know there ever was a concept called freedom? That is our challenge. That is our mission – to assure they do.

Understand that the pillars of freedom – free enterprise, private property and individual liberty – have been proven again and again to be the greatest force of human prosperity and happiness ever devised. Yet the socialism of Sustainable Development has never worked – no matter how many times or different ways it's been tried. Human misery, poverty, and sacrifice have always been its result.

We must take each new assault and overcome it. We must work to help those timid souls to see where this tyranny will lead. We must build a movement and keep fighting no matter the odds against us. The option of defeat is simply too horrible to consider. We have one choice…

Rise and Rise Again Until Lambs Become Lions!

IN CONCLUSION, TWO QUOTES

One confirms that private property is the leading road block to the "Plan" and the urgency of the Sustainable agenda to eliminate the concept through top-down control.

The second clearly illustrates the false premise of the Sustainable argument that redistribution of wealth is the road to fairness, equality and happiness, or that government is the answer.

1. *"What's been hardest is the way our legal system is structured to favor private property. I think people all over this city, of every background, would like to have the city government be able to determine which building goes where, how high it will be, who gets to live in it, what the rent will be."*

New York City Mayor William DeBlasio
(Interview, New York Magazine, September 2017)

1. *"The first lesson of economics is scarcity: there is never enough of anything to fully satisfy all those who want it. The first lesson of politics is to disregard the first lesson of economics."*

Economist Thomas Sowell

INDEX

BIBLIOGRAPHY

Tom DeWeese, Tom. *Agenda 21, The Wrenching Transformation of America*, APC publication, 2017.

C. Gregory Dale, *The Planning Commissioners Guide*, Planners Press, 2013.

Henry Lamb, *The Rise of Global Governance*, Sovereignty International, Inc. Tennessee, 2008.

UNEP, *Global Biodiversity Assessment*, Cambridge Press, 1995.

UNCED, *Earth Summit, Agenda 21*. UN Programme of Acton from Rio, United Nations, 1992.

Alexei Gutnov, et al, *The Ideal Communist City*, Baburov, et al., iPress series on the environment, 1968.

The Commission on Global Governance, *Our Global Neighborhood*, Oxford University Press ,1995.

Jo Hindman, *Blame Metro*, Caxton Press, 1967.

Jo Hindman, *The Metrocrats*, Caxton Press, 1974.

Amatai Etzioni, *New Communitarian Thinking*, University of Virginia Press, 1995.

Philip C. Bom, *The Coming Century of Commonism*, The Beauty and the Beast of Global Governance, Policy Books, Inc., 1992.

The Club of Rome, *The Limits to Growth/Report on the predicament of mankind*, Universe Books, NY, 1972

Michael S, Coffman, PhD., *Plundered, Environmental Perspectives Ink Press*, 2012.

Rose L. Martin, *Fabian Freeway*, Heritage Foundation Press, Chicago, 1966.

Brian Sussman, *Eco-Tyrrany*, WND Books, 2012.

Carroll Quigley, *Tragedy and Hope*, GSG Associates Publishing,1966.

Presidents Council on Sustainable Development, Daniel Sitarz, ed., *Sustainable America*, Earth Press, 1998.

National Research Council, *Sustainability and the U.S. EPA*, National Academy Press, 2011.

Doddes, Felix, ed., *The Way Forward/Beyond Agenda 21*, Earthscan Press, 1997.

Ron Arnold and Alan Gottlieb, *Trashing the Economy/How Runaway Environmentalism is Wrecking America*, Merrill Press, 1994.

G. Edward Griffin, *The Creature from Jekyll Island/A second look at the Federal Reserve*, 1998 .

Patrick M. Wood, *Technocracy Rising/The Trojan Horse of Global Transformation*, Coherent Publications/American Media, 2015.

F'cker County, the Peyton Place of the Piedmont, Dokken, Katherine, Underdog Justice Productions, LLC, 2015.

B.K. Eakman, *How To Counter Group Manipulation Tactics (The Techniques of Unethical Consensus Building Unmasked)*, Midnight Whistler Publishers, 2011.

Maurice Strong, *Where on Earth Are We Going*? Texere, LLC, 2000.

Al Gore, *Earth In The Balance, Ecology and the Human Spirit*, Plume Press,1993.

Joseph L. Bast, Peter J. Hill, and Richard C. Rue, *Eco-Sanity, A Common-Sense Guide to Environmentalism*, Madison Books/ The Heartland Institute, 1994.

Craig D. Idso and Robert M. Carter, *Climate Change Reconsidered II*, Nongovernmental International Panel of Climate Change, The Heartland Institute, 2014.

Robert H. Nelson, *Public Lands and Private Rights: The Failure of Scientific Management*, University Press of America, 1995.

Paul Driessen, *Eco-Imperialism, Green Power Black Death*, The Free Enterprise Press, 2003.

WEBSITES

For maps of the megaregions, phasing of high-speed rail, and other regional planning:
http://www.america2050.org/maps/

The Wildlands Map drawn up by Dr. Michael Coffman:
http://www.freedomadvocates.org/wp-content/uploads/2015/04/Slide-22.jpg

For in-depth information on Affirmatively Furthering Fair Housing:
https://sustainablefreedomlab.org/

For more information than you want to know about Sustainable Development, it's plans, programs, and those who have designed it and are carrying it out:
https://americanpolicy.org/

Smart Meters:
https://stopsmartmeters.org/why-stop-smart-meters/

Library of Liberty:
http://oll.libertyfund.org/pages/books-and-titles

The Constitution:
https://www.archives.gov/founding-docs/constitution-transcript
campconstitution.org
constitutionalalliance.org

The Bill of Rights:
https://www.archives.gov/founding-docs/bill-of-rights-transcript

Hernando de Soto's *The Mystery of Capital*:
https://yendieu.files.wordpress.com/2009/04/the-mystery-of-capital.pdf

Gutnov's *The Ideal Communist City*:
www.americandeception.com/index.php?.../The_Ideal_Communist_
City-Gutnov

Global Warming:
http://www.cfact.org/
http://www.sepp.org/

Technocracy:
www.technocracy.news

28 Page list of UN NGOs as of 2016:
http://undocs.org/E/2016/INF/5

Global Warming;
cfact.org
http://www.climatedepot.com/